Praise for The Ultimate Book of

C000062445

"This book will quickly double and tri|
to decision makers and make more sales-faster!"
- Brian Tracy, Best-selling Author of *Eat That Frog*

"*The Ultimate Book of Phone Scripts* is an amazing resource. If
you need to know what to say in any selling situation, all you have
to do is turn to a page, copy down the word for word script, adapt
it to your selling style, and in an instant you're a Top 20 producer!
Absolutely the best book on phone sales I've seen in a long time.
Buy it, study it and use it to begin profiting from it today."

- Jeffrey J. Fox, NY Times Best-selling Author of
How To Become a Rainmaker

"Mike Brooks has nailed it! Scripts don't tie your hands, they free
you up to take control of the potentially-slippery phone sale. It
doesn't matter if it's a product sale or getting a commitment for
an appointment, preplanned questions help you take control and
get your potential clients talking--telling you what they'll own.
Read this book and you'll win more sales!"

- Tom Hopkins, Author of *How to Master the Art*
of Selling

"Mike Brooks nails it! *The Ultimate Book of Phone Scripts* is
absolutely the best guide for selling over the phone that has ever
been written. This book gives you everything you need to double
your income today!"

- Jeb Blount, Author of *the AMAZON #1 Best-seller:*
People Buy You

Praise for The Ultimate Book of Phone Scripts . . .

"As business to business inside sales takes on a greater role with more sales responsibility for corporate America, so has the need for improvement of virtual selling skills." Mike Brooks', *The Ultimate Book of Phone Scripts*, is a library of excellent tips for call introductions, building rapport, handling objections, etc., which individuals and teams can use to sharpen their sales skills.

- Bob Perkins, CEO of the American Association of Inside Sales Professionals

"'Ring Ring' soon becomes 'Ka Ching' with Mike's new book, *The Ultimate Book of Phone Scripts*. Mike provides you with killer new real world script samples that enable you to find out what it's really going to take to close the sale. If you're ready for your sales to dramatically improve, then pick up this book, pick up the phone, and pick up a lot more profits!"

- Scott Channell, Author of *Setting Sales Appointments*

"Mike Brooks is the real deal when it comes to training on how to use the phone to make money! He is the best at it. His new book, *The Ultimate Book of Phone Scripts* is packed with proven, real world, word for word scripts that will make anyone who sells over the phone instantly better. Buy this book, read it, and follow the techniques and scripts in it. You'll be happy you did!"

- Mike Blinder, President of Blinder Group, Inc. and Author of *Survival Selling*

Praise for The Ultimate Book of Phone Scripts . . .

"Virtually every potential sale begins with a phone call. Unfortunately, very few salespeople (inside or outside) have been properly trained to make these important calls in a highly efficient and effective manner. Mike Brooks, a leading Inside Sales trainer in the US, will show you how to instantly establish rapport, differentiate yourself from all other salespeople calling on that prospect, and build trust and credibility – all within 10 to 15 seconds!

This book should be required reading for every single company with an inside and/or outside sales force. Read this book, master the simple techniques Mike is telling you to do, and you will find yourself in the Top 20%!"

- Peter Lantos, Editor of *The Elite Advisor*™ (www.TheEliteAdvisor.ca)

"I wish this book had been available when I began my selling career. A treasure you will want to keep right next to the phone!"

- Ed Brodow, Author of *Negotiation Boot Camp*

"Mike Brooks has done it again! If you are a salesperson struggling with meeting your quota or competing in this hyper competitive market, *The Ultimate Book of Phone Scripts* will put you over the top. I wholeheartedly recommend Mike's material and have clients that have used his techniques and scripts successfully in their sales organizations. Pick it up today if you want to transform your sales from mediocrity to extraordinary!"

- Marc J. Beauchamp, Author of *How to Survive and Thrive in the Merchant Services Industry*

Praise for The Ultimate Book of Phone Scripts . . .

"When I first met Mike Brooks in 2008, I was not a believer in scripts. He reminded me that even the best professional football teams run plays which are like scripts. I decided to give scripts a shot for my sales team. Not only do my new salespeople ramp quicker by using his scripts, but our average revenue per account has increased by 39% since 2008! No single tool can match these kinds of proven results. Grab this book, use these scripts, and watch your results sky rocket as well!"

- Kevin Gaither, Director of Inside Sales, Business.com

"Every sales person who uses the phone should own this book and refer to it frequently."

**- Dave Kahle, Kahle Way Sales Systems
(www.davekahle.com)**

"Cold calling isn't for the faint hearted. Why? Because most salespeople don't have or use an effective strategy and approach when it comes to this vital skill. Most salespeople just wing it and unfortunately this approach is doomed to fail. If you want to develop a winning approach that works, devour Mike's book. You won't regret it. It's filled with great information that will help you sell more no matter what you sell."

- Tim Connor, CSP, Author of the No. 1 best sales book in the world for over 20 years. *Soft Sell* is in 21 languages with sales over one million copies.

"I have been teaching companies and sales reps how to cold call and set appointments for 20 years and I know that Mike's scripts and techniques in *The Ultimate Book of Phone Scripts* really work. If you need help, then this collection of word for word scripts is just

Praise for The Ultimate Book of Phone Scripts . . .

what you need to succeed in just about any sales situation. Buy the book, learn and use these scripts, and you'll make more sales and income than you ever have before. This is a must have resource for all sales professionals!"

- Wendy Weiss, The Queen of Cold Calling

A must-read, must-own book for anyone who wants to increase their sales right away with less effort and more fun. This book will supercharge your results.

Shon Messer, MSFS,RFC Insurance Professional

The Ultimate Book of Phone Scripts

Mike Brooks

Mr. Inside Sales

Thomson, Georgia

Sales Gravy Press
The Sales Book Publisher™
P.O. Box 1389
Thomson, GA 30824

Published by Sales Gravy Press, an imprint of 3 Palms Publishing
Group, LLC
Printed in the United States of America

Cover Design: Dave Blaker

First Edition

ISBN-13: 9781935602057
ISBN-10: 1-935602-05-5

This book is for any salesperson who has ever dreaded picking up the phone to make a sales call. I know how hard it can be, and I also know that when you begin using these proven scripts you'll once again remember why you got into sales to begin with...

Table of Contents

Table of Contents

Foreword

by Jeb Blount
Author of *People Buy You*

While attending a conference recently a fan of my Sales Guy Podcasts walked up to me and asked, "Do you think outside sales is dead?" The question set me back on my heels for a moment. I've been in outside sales my entire career and the last thing I wanted to ponder was the demise of my chosen profession.

But then I thought back to January of 2009. The Great Recession was kicking into high gear. Our customers were slashing their advertising spending and suddenly cost reduction became a front and center issue for my company (SalesGravy.com). One of the easiest expenses to control was travel and entertainment. The fear, however, was that cutting travel would cut sales since we did so much of our selling and relationship building face to face. However, faced with a dire economy we challenged ourselves to save money by selling over the phone rather than traveling to see our customers and prospects in person.

I'll admit that I was afraid that we would not be effective and would lose sales. I'm happy to say that I was wrong. Our sales actually increased. I personally closed more than $3 million in new business without ever visiting a client for a face to face meeting.

Why Selling Over the Phone Works

The number one reason for our success is that we became more efficient. We could cover far more ground over the phone, therefore, we were engaged with more accounts and developed a larger pipeline. We also found that sales meetings by phone took far less time than in-person meetings. That afforded us more time to research and qualify prospects, which meant that when we were on the phone, we were engaged with more qualified buyers.

Telephone Meetings are Good for Customers

Another key reason for our success was that our buyers appreciated the time savings as well. In fact, it was far easier to set an appointment for an online demo than an in-person meeting. With the recession, buyers were taking on greater responsibilities. As the head count at their companies was slashed, they had less time to spend meeting with salespeople. Telephone meetings made it easier for them to take time out of their day to listen to our presentations. We quickly discovered that they appreciated that we were willing to meet with them over the phone.

In the end we traveled less, sold more, saved lots of money and improved our quality of life. However, this did not mean that outside sales was dead.

We still got on planes and into cars to visit customers. Getting face to face with clients is still the most powerful means of building and anchoring relationships. We also had a few prospects who demanded a face to face meeting. In both cases, because we had done so much work on the phone beforehand, our face to face meetings were more effective and allowed us to develop deeper relationships. We have saved so much money on travel that we have been able to invest more in marketing and trade shows--where we have the chance to meet many of our clients and potential clients face to face in an informal environment.

Learning to Effectively Sell Over the Phone

One of our first moves when we changed our strategy to spend more time on the phone and less time in face to face sales calls was to require our entire sales team to read Mike Brooks's book *The Real Secrets of the Top 20%: How to Double Your Income Selling Over the Phone.* At first our reps complained that the book was written for inside salespeople and did not apply to outside sales. It did not take long for them to see how the techniques and skills Mike teaches in *Real Secrets of the Top 20%* is applicable to anyone in the sales profession.

The fact is, if you are in outside sales you can become more efficient, effective, and close more business by learning how to sell over the phone. And if you are already selling over the phone, Mike's techniques and proven strategies will end much of your daily frustration, help you close more deals and ultimately be happier in your sales job.

The Real Secret to Selling Over the Phone

Selling over the phone is more difficult than selling in person because you cannot observe body language. Because of this, listening is the key to becoming great at selling over the phone. You must develop the self-discipline to remain completely focused on your prospect and avoid distractions. When you listen you will find that you build amazing connections with your buyers and uncover real problems that lead to closed deals.

Most salespeople have a difficult time really listening while on the phone with a prospect or customer because they spend the vast majority of their time thinking about the next thing they are going to say. This results in a failure to pick up cues and clues that lead to sales.

This is why Mike Brooks points out that the top 20% producers use scripts. Why? A practiced script makes their voice intonation, speaking style, and flow sound professional. It also helps them sound competent and knowledgeable. Scripts have the added benefit of freeing your mind to focus on your message and your audience rather than on the words you use. And scripts work so well in sales because we have many repetitive activities, like making cold calls, setting appointments, making follow-up calls, giving elevator speeches, offering product demos, answering questions, making presentations, overcoming objections, and making closes.

When you have a script, you never have to worry about what to say.

Why Using a Script Helps

If you really want to observe the power of scripts, just notice the difference in a politician when he is speaking off script. You will notice when he is giving a speech with a teleprompter, which is a script, he is incredibly convincing. But without a script, he often stumbles on his words and makes many of the same mistakes we make in normal conversation. Scripts are what make most politicians compelling personalities.

However, when I stand in front of a group of salespeople and utter the word "script," the first thing I usually hear are groans. In the face of the overwhelming evidence that scripts work in sales, most salespeople still reject them off hand.

I hear all of the regular excuses, including my favorite, "I don't sound like myself when I use a script."

To that I answer, "Good, that is the whole point. The primary objective of the script is to make you sound different and to project a professional message."

The rebuttal is always the same: "But you don't understand, Jeb. I'll sound canned."

Scripts Don't Have to Make You Sound Canned

The fear of sounding canned is legitimate. If actors and politicians sounded canned, TV shows and movies wouldn't be entertaining and speeches wouldn't be believable. But that is exactly why actors, politicians, and top sales professionals rehearse and practice. They work and work until the script sounds natural and becomes *their* voice.

This is what most salespeople don't get. Whether it is a big presentation or a routine call to set an appointment, the words that come out of your mouth must be practiced to make the best impression on your prospect or customer. Scripts are a powerful way to manage your message, but they must be rehearsed.

When salespeople complain that scripts make them sound canned, what they are really saying is, "I'm too lazy," or "I don't care enough about my own success to take time to write my script and rehearse it." They are willing to shoot from the hip and bet their quota and income on the roll of the dice. Sadly, this is the exact reason that the top 20% of sales professionals make 80% of the commissions. They are simply willing to do the things that average salespeople are unwilling to do.

Mike Brooks to the Rescue

I've spent more than twenty years in sales. Over the years I've sold for multiple companies, been a sales manager, vice president of sales, sales trainer, speaker, and author. When it comes to sales, I've "Been there, done that and have the t-shirts to prove it." In all those years, I've never met anyone like Mike Brooks. In my opinion, he is the world's top authority on selling over the phone. If you want double your income, listen to Mike.

This book truly is the Ultimate Book of Phone Scripts. It is a secret weapon that will leapfrog you ahead of your competitors and peers. When you make these scripts a regular part of your call routine and sales process, I can unequivocally guarantee that you will become a top 20% producer.

The question you must answer though, is "Am I committed to being my best?" If the answer is yes then this book will change everything for you.

Can you really close deals using scripts? The answer is yes. I've learned firsthand that when practicing the right techniques, you can close deals anywhere you can find a quiet place with a phone and internet connection.

Jeb Blount, Author of the Amazon #1 bestseller, *People Buy You: The Real Secret to What Matters Most in Business*

Introduction

The Power of Phone Scripts

I remember all those years ago sitting at my desk, staring at a stack of leads and looking at my phone with nothing but dread. After I'd procrastinated as much as I could, I would reluctantly pick up the phone, dial the number, and grimace as the gatekeeper answered: "Who's calling?" "What company are you with?" "Will he know what this call is about?" Those uncomfortable gatekeeper questions not only screened me out, but inevitably left me wishing I had gone into any line of work but sales. Of course this was just the first call of the day and I had hundreds more cold calls like this to make before the weekend. It made my stomach hurt just thinking about it.

For months I struggled along like this literally hating my job. Right before I was about to walk out the door and quit, I met a sales trainer who changed everything. I'll never forget when he pulled out a big notebook of scripts and told me that the only way I would ever be consistently successful was if I learned and followed a proven system and sales process. He explained that phone scripts were central to cold calling, setting appointments, follow-up calls, and closing sales over the phone.

Scripts? Are you kidding? I don't want to sound like a telemarketer!

That was my first reaction when he began talking about scripts. Like all of us, I got calls at night from telemarketers selling newspapers and raising money, and the last thing I wanted was to sound like one of them. But then he said something that made sense. He said that if you really thought about it, every true professional followed a script or a carefully practiced routine. Whether you were a professional athlete who practiced scripted plays and techniques, or dancers who worked hard at perfecting exact moves over and over, what made all these professionals successful was that they found the most effective way to do something, they practiced it over and over, and then, when it was their turn to perform, they concentrated on delivering the most polished, mistake-free performance of their career.

I could buy that in terms of athletes, but scripting out what I was going to say? That seemed a bit much. And that's when he reminded me of actors who get paid millions of dollars per film. They don't get in front of the camera or on stage and begin ad-libbing their lines, do they? Never! Instead, each line has been carefully scripted and rehearsed, so that when delivered, the actor sounds natural, sincere, and believable. Rather than stumble around wondering what they are going to say next, these highly paid professionals are able to concentrate on their timing, delivery, pacing, volume, tone, and inflection of their voice.

However, I was still skeptical and uncomfortable with the whole concept of scripting my calls. So he asked me if I had ever felt a transfer of emotion – either feeling happy or sad, or any other strong emotion - after seeing a good movie. I nodded yes. "Did you stop to realize that you were just watching an actor deliver a set of scripted lines?" He asked. He then explained that well over 70% (some will even claim over 90%!) of any sale is simply a transfer of conviction and enthusiasm, and the best way to do this is to concentrate on your delivery of information, rather than on what you are going to say about it next.

He had my attention. When I got out of that training, I was committed to at least trying scripts. It was the best decision I ever made. My sales and income soared! After being one of the worst producers in the company, in just nine months I became the top producer, and that year I earned a six-figure income. I attribute it all to using carefully crafted scripts, and I've spent my career writing, perfecting, and teaching other sales professionals how to use scripts to overcome objections, set more qualified appointments, close more sales, and move into the top 20% of the producers in their companies and industries.

Six Reasons to Use Scripts

If you're still not convinced you should be using scripts, then I'd like to present the six main benefits to using effective and proven scripts. They are:

1. The more closely you follow a script, the more professional you will sound. How many times have you heard the salesperson next to you ramble on and on, making things up as they go along because they are not using a script? Have you ever noticed how each call they make sounds different and a little worse than the one before it? *Sometimes you wonder if the prospect is still on the other end of the phone.* The fact is, the more you ramble on, the less control you have of the conversation, the less qualifying you are doing, and the more you sound like the telemarketers who call and bug you at night. If you enjoy splitting up 20% of the sales and income earned in your company or industry, then you can go on winging it.

If, on the other hand, you truly want to be a top professional and earn your share of 80% of the money being made, then you have to sound like a professional, and that will only happen by following a script or format. If you are not already doing so, then you need to begin using a script or format today.

2. Following a script will ensure that you ask all the right qualifying questions. How many times have you gotten off the phone after winging your way through a qualifying call only to discover that you didn't have important information, such as:

• How many other decision makers are there?

• Where exactly is the money going to come from to buy your product or service?

• Who do they usually buy from and why?

- Are they getting a bid or quote from that company as well?

- How many other solutions are they looking at?

- Are they in the market to purchase your product or service now, or do they have to wait three to six months?

These and many other important qualifying questions are oftentimes never asked, because when you are not following a script or format, you are too busy trying to think up what you are going to say next, and you forget to ask what is really important.

The real problem comes, though, when you call these unqualified prospects back, because that is when you pay the price for not getting this information in the first place. How many times have you called back a prospect only to be blown off the phone with any combination of the following: "We looked at it and we're just not interested." Or, "I'm not in the market now, but maybe six months down the line you can call again." Or, "Oh, I could never afford this now; I only took the information because you said you would send it!"

Frustrating, isn't it? If these are common responses you get when you call your prospects back, then it is time you start sticking to a script so that when you are on qualifying calls, you cover all the important points and don't miss information that will come back and sabotage the sale later.

3. Scripts make your job easy. Let's face it – you already know 90% of the objections your prospects and clients use, don't you? You get them so often that at times it seems like *they* are following a script! If you know what is coming, why not be prepared for it in advance and handle it like a professional? Rather than have that sick feeling in your gut when you get an objection, wouldn't you rather be able to relax and handle those old, tired objections with rebuttals that can cut through smokescreens and help you close the sale?

Scripts allow you to do just that. Being prepared for the objections that you get day in and day out will not only make your job easier, but it will make you more successful as well. Think about it: When you get the standard, "The price is too high" objection, wouldn't it feel better to say:

"I understand. Let's put the price aside for a moment. If the price was more in alignment with what you were willing/able to spend, would this be something you would seriously consider moving forward with today?"

Now doesn't that sound better than all the things you may be saying right now? Believe me, 80% of your competition ad-lib and make things up when they get this and other similar objections, and it only makes their job harder. By being prepared with scripts like this that work, you'll be prepared, confident, and you'll easily be able to handle the smokescreens and objections that are not only frustrating, but costing you thousands of dollars in lost sales right now.

4. You will be free to truly listen to what your prospect is trying to tell you. Rather than wondering what you are going to say next, you will be able to carefully listen to what a prospect is telling you, and how they are saying it. You will find that if you listen carefully enough, a prospect will always tell you what you will need to do or say to make the sale (and/or why they are not ready to buy yet).

This is a very important point. Many times while qualifying, if you are following a script or outline and asking the right questions and listening to your prospect's responses, you will be amazed by what your prospect will reveal. They will often tell you exactly what it is going to take to close them, or what they stay away from and the reasons they won't buy. Either way, wouldn't it be nice to know in advance exactly what it is going to take to close your prospect when you call them back? You will only be able to hear this if you are carefully listening, rather than being preoccupied with what you are going to say next.

5. Following scripts gives you confidence. You will find that cold calling, appointment setting and closing actually get easier when you follow scripts, because you will hear the same objections so many times you won't be thrown off. As you make hundreds of calls, you will find that there is very little creativity in the world of objections. Almost 90% of initial resistance statements are the same. Things like, "I'm not interested," or "We don't have the budget," or "We already have a supplier," are probably things you hear dozens of times a week don't you?

By following a script and using rebuttals that work, you will be able to handle these objections with confidence and overcome the initial obstacles that frustrate 80% of the salespeople who are winging it by coming up with a different rebuttal to the same old objections every time.

6. When following a script or outline each time you make a call, you will be able to practice perfection. Most people say that practice makes perfect, but that isn't true. Instead: Practice makes permanent. Only practice of perfection makes perfect! If you are not following scripts each time you call, then you are continuing to practice bad habits and most likely you are not improving at all. In fact, you are probably sounding worse and worse and wondering what is wrong.

On the other hand, if you are following scripts, then each time you speak with a prospect or client you are getting better on each call. With each objection you get, you become stronger and grow more confident, because you are practicing perfection.

Scripts also allow you to perfect the delivery of your voice: The timing, inflection, pacing, enthusiasm, tone, etc. The way you open a conversation, the way you qualify, the way you close, the way you ask for the order, even the way you respond to objections is basically the same each time, so doesn't it make sense to learn and practice the most effective techniques available? Of course it does! It is the practice of these basic techniques that will elevate you to the Top 20% of the Sales Professionals at your company.

The 80/20 Rule in Sales

If you've been in sales any length of time, then you've heard about the 80/20 rule in sales. Quite simply, 80% of the sales and income is made by the Top 20% producers, while the other 80% of salespeople struggle to close sales and cut up the remaining 20%. No matter what company or industry I work with, I can always find the top producers, and I'll bet that you can point them out in your company as well. If you're in the 80% category and you are struggling to make sales, then I'm sure you're asking yourself what you can do to move into that elite Top 20% group. The answer is simple: Be prepared with and start using effective and proven scripts.

One of the things you'll find without fail is that Top 20% producers are successful because they are prepared in advance for the objections, resistance and put-offs they get over and over again. Compare this with the bottom 80% who ad-lib their responses to common objections and struggle with the selling situations they are in day after day. Using the carefully worded scripts in this book will immediately help you in the selling situations that are frustrating you now, and they will improve your ability to handle the blow-offs and objections you get from both qualified and unqualified prospects alike.

For example, let's take the common objection of, "I'm going to have to show this to (my boss, my manager, my partner, etc.). Eighty percent of so called closers will answer this objection in dozens of different ways, and often all in the same week! Their answers include things like, "Well, ah, when do you think they will look at it?" And, "Do you think he/she would be available now?" And, "I thought you mentioned you were the decision maker on this?"

Given this same objection, the Top 20%, who are prepared with proven and effective scripts, know how to isolate this worn out smokescreen and reply, "Great. And let me ask you something. If (your partner, boss, manager, etc.) say they like it and tell you to do what you think is best, what would your decision be on this today?"

As you will discover while reading this book, the best way to handle many common objections is not to answer them, but rather to first question and isolate them to determine if they are real objections.

The Ultimate Book of Phone Scripts is packed with hundreds of proven scripts and techniques that Top 20% producers use to dominate your company and industry. The good news is that as soon as you start using them, you'll move into that Top 20% group, too!

How to Use This Book

You will find hundreds of word-for-word scripts in this book that will help you deal with most of the resistance, smokescreens, objections, and selling situations you encounter every day. While many of the scripts may be used exactly as they are, I encourage you to work with them and adapt them to fit your product or service and your selling style. Don't be afraid to rewrite them to better fit how you sell. Just be sure to use them over and over again so you perfect your delivery and sound natural.

Eventually, your goal is to internalize your scripts (memorize them), so when you get an objection or blow-off, you can handle it easily and concentrate on the delivery of your response. Once you get comfortable with the scripts that work best for you, one of the things you'll find is that using scripts will make selling enjoyable. You will no longer be surprised, discouraged or frustrated by objections.

Once you begin selling with confidence, you will find that your new attitude is contagious. Your prospects and clients will respond to your enthusiasm. You will enter each selling situation with the expectant attitude of closing the sale. This is how top producers think and act, and it is this attitude that will propel you into the Top 20%.

Where to Go for More Help on Inside Sales

This book is packed with scripts, questions and closes that will immediately improve how you sound and sell over the phone. The scripts in this book will put more money in your pocket the moment you begin using them. Whether you are new to sales or have been at it for years, you will perform better and with less effort when you use these scripts.

Because this book is primarily designed to provide you with word-for-word scripts, you may want to learn more about the strategies, techniques, and philosophies behind what it takes to become a top 20% producer selling over the phone. You may be interested in these additional resources.

- **Book:** *The Real Secrets of the Top 20%*
- **5-CD Series:** How to Double Your Income Selling Over the Phone.
- **MP3 Download:** The Ultimate Secrets of the Top 20%

I highly recommend you invest in my comprehensive selling system today. You can find it by visiting my website:

www.MrInsideSales.com

1 | Cold Calling Scripts

Cold calling. The very mention of it sends shivers down the backs of even the most seasoned sales professionals. And why shouldn't it? If you've had to pick up the phone to prospect, set an appointment or cold call someone, you know the horrible feelings of rejection you get when someone tells you they aren't interested, or, worse, that you should take their number off your calling list and never call there again!

When you think about it, who can blame them? You know what it's like to be cold called at home or your office and then to have some sales rep barrage you with their sales pitch. This is how most salespeople open their calls, and it's why most of them are shut down almost immediately.

In this section you are going to learn how to actually connect with your prospect first (what a concept, I know), and how to deal with the brush-offs and blow-offs that make cold calling so miserable.

How to Open a Cold Call

In sales you have about 10 to 15 seconds to make a first impression. Unfortunately, most salespeople make that impression in about two seconds, and it's usually a bad one. They do it most often

1

by uttering these dreaded words: *"How are you today?"*

Nothing makes you stand out as a typical telemarketer or salesperson more than the insincere opening - *How are you today?* (which is how 80% of your competition delivers it). If you want to separate yourself from your competition and actually connect to your prospect, then NEVER ask "How are you today?" Instead use any of these openings after you say your name and company:

Five Best Cold Call Openings

1. **"Happy Monday!"** (Or Wednesday, or Thursday, whatever day it is). This is my personal favorite. Before you laugh it off as being cheesy, I encourage you to try it. This technique works well because it immediately changes the frame of mind of the person you're speaking with. You will be amazed by how this opens both gatekeepers and prospects up, and gets them to relate and respond to you in a natural and sincere way.

This opening sets an easy and natural tone for the rest of the call, and it puts your prospect at ease just long enough for you to move to the next part of your call.

2. **"Is it raining there, too?"** (Or hot or foggy, etc.). Immediately connecting with your prospect on an issue unrelated to sales takes the pressure off and usually gets them talking. Let's face it, we're all just people, and by starting a conversation with a topic others can relate to, you'll be establishing a connection and separating yourself from all the other cold callers.

3. **"I'm so glad I reached you, I need a little bit of help. Are you the person who handles XYZ?"** Or, "I'm supposed to speak to the person in charge of your receivables, do you happen to know who that is, please?"

This is a great technique because you are immediately making someone feel important and helpful. And who doesn't like to feel that way? In addition, by coming right out and letting the other person know why you are calling, you are differentiating yourself from all the other sales reps who are calling and trying to trick their way to the prospect. Don't forget to use the 'please' at the end!

4. "How's your day going?" This is a very effective alternative to "How are you today?" It only works if you are sincere and actually listen to how their day is going. Listen carefully and respond accordingly with something like, "Gee, I know what you mean..."

5. "Can you hear me OK?" While this opening may seem a little abrupt, it actually works on several levels. First, it almost always elicits a yes response, and next it gets your prospect to pay attention and to really listen. Used at the right time and with the right prospect, it's a great way to control the opening of a call.

These five techniques will separate you from your competition and get your prospects to drop their guard and become receptive to what you say next. Work with them this week and find the ones you are most comfortable with. You will love the new feeling and space you create at the opening of your cold calls.

Opening Statements: What To Do and What Not To Do

Once you have made a great first impression on your prospect, you have a very brief window (about 10 seconds) to engage them and assess their level of interest. One of the biggest mistakes to avoid at this point is delivering a long monologue about what you do (the most common mistake cold callers make). Likewise, you want to avoid asking them a closed-ended question that only sets you up for a negative response, i.e., the following:

Prospect: "Hi this is Bob, can I help you?"

Sales Rep: "Oh hi, this is Brad Smith with the XYZ company, have you ever heard of us?"

- Or -

"Oh hi, this is Brad Smith with the XYZ company, do you have a few minutes now?"

Because Brad is starting the call off with a closed-ended question, he gives his prospect an immediate opportunity to get rid of him: "No, I don't have time, good bye." or "No, I've never heard of you, I really don't have time to talk now." If you are using either of these close-ended openings, stop doing so today.

Another opening that will quickly get your cold call off track is an attempt to trick the gatekeeper to put you through:

Gatekeeper: "Can I tell him who is calling?"

Sales Rep: "Yes, tell him it's Brad."

Gatekeeper: "Does he know you?"

Sales Rep: "Yep, we've spoken before."

Gatekeeper: "Can I tell him what this call is about?"

Sales Rep: "Yeah. He asked me to keep in touch with him."

- Or -

"I'm calling him back."

Both of these responses are often blatant lies, but it's amazing how salespeople justify them with the reasoning, "Well he gets a lot of calls; he won't remember," Or "Well, I make a lot of calls, and I did call him two months ago." Of course they never reached him, but that doesn't stop them from lying about it.

If you are using methods to trick your prospect or gatekeeper, please stop them immediately. There is a better way...

Two Cold Call Openings You DO Want To Use

I was consulting with a company a few years ago when I received a cold call that was so honest, so refreshing, I recruited the guy to come work for me on the spot! Here's how it went:

Cold Call Opening #1:

Mike: "Hi this is Mike, how can I help you?"

Rep: "Hi Mike, this is _____ _____ with the XYZ company. Mike, we have never spoken before and I don't mean to barge into your day, but I represent a company and a product that I think could be very beneficial to you. It has to do with your lead tracking system, and all my clients are happy they took a moment to listen. Can I run a few details by you now to see if there's a fit?"

Now that was different – honest, respectful, and it contained a value statement for the prospect which encouraged them listen.

Cold Call Opening #2:

"Hi Bob, this is Mike Brooks with Mr. Inside Sales, how's your (Tuesday or day of the week) going so far?" *[Listen carefully here to how and what your prospect says!]* Bob, I know you're busy so I'll be brief....I see you visited my Inside Sales Training website, and I wanted to find out what kind of help you were looking for in regards to your inside sales team?"

At this point I shut up and listen to not only what they say, but to how they say it. Now, obviously, I'm calling back a warm lead, so here's how you handle a cold one:

"Bob, I know you're busy so I'll make this brief. I got your name from (name your lead source – paper, association, list, etc.) and I see you manage an inside sales team. Now we've not spoken before but I've sat in your chair for many years and I understand many of the challenges you're probably facing right now. Let me ask you a quick question – if I could give you some free resources that will help your team sell more and avoid rejection, would you be interested in downloading them today?"

Those people who blow me off are not buyers, and those who listen and respond are potential clients. This is an important point. Most salespeople feel compelled to turn everyone they speak with into a prospect and get information out to them no matter what (the old "Fill your pipeline" mentality). But top 20% producers understand that most people aren't going to be deals and they would rather ask a direct question, listen to what and how the prospect responds and move on if they aren't interested. I might try one or two more qualifying questions (depending on how receptive the prospect is), but if I keep getting a road block, I'll either use the "Next in line" script that you'll read about later, or I will politely excuse myself and make another call.

When you have this type of mindset, and you use these scripts, suddenly prospecting, cold calling and speaking with prospects is easy. If you are struggling now and are either afraid or frustrated by the phone, then chances are you aren't prepared and you are trying too hard. If so, then take some time and adapt these scripts to fit your product or service and your selling style, and get ready to sell naturally and easily!

Three Techniques to Instantly Establish Interest

Because you only have a few precious seconds to make a connection and establish interest, you must have an effective opening prepared in advance. Besides being very busy, your prospects get lots of sales calls - many of them from your direct competition. So why would they want to talk to you? What can you do to separate yourself from all the other calls they get?

The answer is that you have to establish a real connection with your prospect and stop sounding like all the other sales reps who call them. Here is what your competition usually sounds like (**Note: Don't do this!**):

> *"Oh hi Mr. _____, this is _____ _____ with the MLT Group. _____, we are an industry supply manufacturer and we help companies streamline their production process. We work with many companies in your field and save them between 10 to 15% on the cost of their storage and delivery process. What I'd like to do is ask you some questions to see how our process may save you that kind of money as well. Where are you currently getting your..."*

Do you see how this opening makes no connection with the prospect? Do you see how it just starts pitching at the prospect and doesn't acknowledge that the prospect might be busy, or not interested? Do you see how there is no rapport built here and how it's a one sided conversation? How do you feel when someone barges in on your day and starts in with a pitch like this? You're thinking what most prospects are thinking: "How do I get this sales rep off the phone?"

Now let's look at the right way to open your call. Your goal in the first few seconds is to make a connection and get them to interact. You have to acknowledge that they may be busy or state that you respect their time, and you need to establish some rapport and separate yourself from all the other salespeople calling them. Here are three techniques that allow you to instantly establish a connection and generate interest:

Opening Technique #1: Acknowledge that you know your prospect gets a lot of calls -- this will immediately help you establish a connection because you will be saying exactly what they're thinking and feeling. Use:

"Hi _____ this is _____ _____ with (your company). How is your Tuesday (use day of the week) going? Great. Listen _____ __, I know you probably get a ton of calls so I'll make this brief."

Now go into a one to two sentence explanation of why you're calling and what it means to them. Adapt the opening below:

Opening Technique #2: Quickly state your value proposition and ask a qualifying question.

"_____, we provide/service/work with (companies like yours) helping them service/provide/process/do better at _____. Let me ask you a quick question..."

Ask a specific qualifying question tied with a value statement here. Something like:

"If I could show you a way to increase the number of leads you're getting right now and show you how you can easily afford to do so, would you be willing to invest 5 minutes to find out how?"

It's important to listen to not only what they say here, but how they say it. Most of the time you'll be able to tell if you have an interested prospect or not, and after you read a bit more of this section on cold calling, you'll know exactly what to do with both kinds of prospects.

Opening 3: Immediately ask a qualifying question to get them involved. Try:

"Hi _____, this is _____ _____ with (your company). How is your Monday (use day of the week) going? Great. _____, I know you probably get a ton of calls so I'll make this brief. Let me ask you, if I could show you a better way of tracking and shipping and save you money doing it, would it be worth spending five minutes with me next week to show you how?"

- Or -

"What is the one thing you could change that would have a dramatic impact on your productivity and that would save your department money?"

- Or -

"If you had a magic wand and could change one thing about how you currently do (their business), what would it be?"

Can you see how this quick questioning approach is more effective than what you may currently be using now? Eighty percent of your competition still barge in on their prospects and open their calls up with a long explanation about what they do and what they offer, and pitch their products and services without checking in with their prospects or establishing any kind of connection. No wonder most people brush them off the phone!

You can separate yourself from this group instantly, starting today, by using the techniques above. Once again, adapt them to fit your product or service, and then practice them until they are natural and easy for you to use. As you do, you will notice that you struggle less and make more connections with interested and qualified buyers. You will also gain more confidence and feel better about yourself. Just like the top 20% do.

Three Ways to Build Rapport in 30 Seconds

In today's economy where prospects are quick with the brush off, you must find a way to instantly establish rapport, differentiate yourself and build trust and credibility for yourself and your company – and all within about ten seconds!

Here are three additional techniques that will create a sense of ease with your prospects, build real rapport, and get the person on the other end of the phone to trust you.

1.   Resist the urge to cut your prospect off – especially if they are giving you an initial negative response. Again, your prospects get a lot of calls and they are good at blowing you off the phone, and are quick to do so. One problem 80% of sales reps make is that they cut their prospects off as soon as they begin to object, or they start arguing with their prospect's initial blow off response. A better way is to hear your prospect out and be prepared to agree with them by having a scripted response that anticipates and deals with their initial resistance. Try:

" I understand _____, and I'm not calling to sell you anything today. Rather, I'm here to see if there might be a fit between our two companies and if there is, to offer you an additional resource you might be able to use later on. Let me ask you..."

Hearing your prospect out, agreeing with them, and then offering a non-threatening value statement instantly allows your prospect to be heard, and distinguishes you from the other sales reps who are jumping all over them.

2.   Empathize with your prospect by asking how they are dealing with the economy. Hey, let's face it, we're all in the same boat regarding whatever is happening in the economy, and if you're feeling the strain, so is your prospect. Rather than try to bulldoze them, why not empathize with them and try to see things from their perspective?

"I completely understand _____. By the way, how are you dealing with the economy these days?"

- Or -

"I'm sure it's rough for you as well, tell me, how are you making things work in this business climate?"

- Or -

"I'm with you. How long have you been working in that position? What changes have you had to make to survive in today's economy?"

Getting your prospect talking by showing genuine interest will go a long way towards building trust and credibility for yourself and your company.

3. Be prepared to be positive. At the end of a phone call – no matter how short – one party's attitude will have been transferred to the other. Unfortunately, the prospect's negative doom and gloom attitude usually infects the bottom 80% of sales reps. That's why it is so hard for them to pick up the phone.

The top 20%, on the other hand, understand this, are prepared for their prospect's negative responses and attitudes, and make it their goal to enter the call on a positive note and to transfer their positive, enthusiastic attitude to their prospect by the end of the call. They do this by being prepared with positive statements they use in response to the negativity they get all day long.

Prospect: "We're not spending any money on that right now."

Rep: "Some companies aren't, but there are many who recognize that this is the ideal time to capture market share and position themselves for the economic upturn that is coming. Let me ask you this – if you saw a way to earn an immediate ROI on just a small investment, where could you clear up $____ to take advantage of it?"

- Or -

Prospect: "In today's economy I'm just lucky to have a job!"

Rep: "I know what you mean, and if you want to keep that job, now's the time to be proactive and show some real initiative. Here's what other managers I'm speaking with are doing to strengthen their position and build even more value in their services....."

By being prepared with positive statements to the constant negativity you encounter while making cold calls, you not only stay positive yourself, but also transfer that vibe to others. When your attitude and enthusiasm improve, clients and prospects will enjoy hearing from you, and you'll begin writing more business and you'll become a magnet for good news and good results.

One Sentence to Establish Immediate Rapport

If you have to make a lot of prospecting calls as part of your sales process – either to set appointments or to find qualified prospects to sell your products and services to - then you know how hard it is to overcome initial resistance and establish rapport. People don't like to be bothered by a sales rep they don't know.

Think about your own reaction when you get a call at home from a telemarketer you don't know. As soon as they begin their pitch, your eyes roll and you start thinking of ways to get off the phone. Even if they are personable (which is rare) or have something you're actually interested in (which is rarer), most of these sales calls feel like an intrusion.

One of the biggest reasons for this is that most sales reps making calls have no idea how to engage a prospect and make a connection in the initial seconds of a call. Making that connection is the most important thing you can do to lower or eliminate initial resistance and give yourself a real chance to see if what you're offering is a fit for the person you're speaking with.

Here is the one sentence you can use that will give you the best chance to make that connection:

"Hi _____, this is _____ _____. We haven't spoken yet but I'm calling you because you (use our product or could benefit from it) and I have (your product offering or benefit) and wanted to run something by you. Let me ask you a quick question, if I could..."

The power in this technique is that by leveling with your prospect that you don't know them, you are immediately eliminating the natural resistance that is there when this goes unspoken. Prospects respect this honesty, and you'll feel a natural connection form as a result.

Don't underestimate the power of this technique. Try it for a few days and see for yourself how effective it is. Obviously, you'll want to adapt it to fit your product or service, but taking the time to do this will pay big dividends.

Remember – making an immediate connection is the most important thing you can do, and this technique will help you do that.

How to Build Relevant Rapport

Let's elaborate on the concept of rapport here. Most salespeople think that talking about the latest sports scores or schmoozing about vacation spots is how you build rapport over the phone. That's totally wrong. In fact doing this just lengthens the call, dilutes your message, and gets you no closer to the deal than you were before you wasted all that time.

If you want to truly connect to your prospect and build the kind of rapport that will actually influence and lead to a closed deal, then you need to learn how to build what I call, "*Relevant*

Rapport." Relevant rapport means taking the time to talk about work related issues your prospect is going through or what they're trying to solve, and then expanding on these relevant issues and letting them know you understand exactly what they're trying to accomplish and explaining how you are uniquely qualified to help them.

Remember, your prospects have a need. They are looking to you to help them fulfill that need. The more they feel you understand their needs and can help them, the more likely it is they will do business with you. So, how do you build relevant rapport? You start by asking questions related to their specific work related situation. Instead of asking *"So where did you go on vacation?"* ask:

"Now that you're back from vacation, I'll bet you've got lots to catch up on. How can I help you?"

- Or -

"You're probably buried now that you're back from vacation. I'd be happy to refill your normal order from last month and take that bit of business off your plate. Would you like me to send you the same amount as last month?"

Instead of asking *"Are you excited about the upcoming football season?"* ask:

"As we head into the fall, what are your top three priorities for ending the year strong?"

Then layer by asking:

"You know _____, I'm working with another client who has the same goal this quarter. What I proposed for him is to (then explain your solution). Do you think that might help you as well?"

The point of relevant rapport is that your prospect will like you more and trust you more if you show an interest in their problems related to business, rather than their activities outside of business. Just remember that your prospect is under just as much pressure to do their job as you are to do yours. Ask yourself: *Who would you be more interested in talking to – a prospect who wants to talk about the latest diet, or a prospect who wants to place an order?*

I challenge you this week to go out and begin connecting with your prospects on issues related to what they are doing for 8 to 9 hours a day – trying to get their jobs done. When you can show them how to do that better, faster or easier, then you will have truly made the connection with them that counts the most. That's what building real rapport is all about.

Five Ways to Sound More Natural On the Phone

I don't know about you but I can always tell when a telemarketer is cold calling me. From the moment they begin speaking, "Hi is this Mr. Brooks?" to the way they mechanically read their scripts, I have them pegged before they get past their first sentence. And, same as you, I am immediately not interested.

If you are reading this book, it probably means you have to pick up the phone – either to make appointments, call prospects back, return calls to clients, etc. – and if so, then you need to learn how to sound natural on the phone and avoid putting your prospects, gatekeepers, assistants, etc. on notice that you're trying to sell something.

To be more effective on the phone you must learn to sound like you're not selling anything. You do this by learning how to disarm prospects, sound natural yet professional, and how to be friendly without being phony. Use these five techniques not only to sound natural on the phone, but also to close more business:

1.   Always use the prospect's first name.   I know that there are two schools of thought on this, one being that you should show respect for someone you don't know and so use either Mr. or Mrs., but I don't agree. I think you can show respect for someone by being courteous and professional, and I think you're going to make a lot more progress if you use a person's first name. Here are the two reasons to do so:

a. First, by using a person's first name you aren't immediately signaling that you are a sales person! How do you feel when someone you don't know calls you and addresses you by "Mr." or "Mrs."? Also, when you use a person's first name, you are starting the call on equal footing, without giving them all the power.

b. Second, everyone likes the sound of their own name. In fact, psychologists have found that everyone's favorite word is their first name! By starting with that you are immediately making a connection, and a personal one at that.

2.   Be polite. You'd be surprised by how many sales reps still try to trick or get around gatekeepers and assistants, and how many are even rude in doing so. Always, always use "please" and "thank you" when speaking with anyone over the phone (or in person for that matter).

Words like "please" and "thank you" go a long way when trying to make a connection with a prospect, and they work especially well when you're trying to get through a gatekeeper. Examine your current scripts now and do all you can to insert the proper courtesies.

3.   Be brief. Most reps go into pitch mode the moment they reach their prospect. It's no surprise prospects can't wait to get off the phone. I review scripts all the time that are essentially a dissertation of a company's brochure. You can turn that around and sound so much better with a brief presentation and checking in with your prospect. Try these scripts:

"Briefly _____, the reason I'm calling is that we've been working with many companies like yours, and I just wanted to see if we could help you as well. Can I ask you just a couple of questions to see if we'd be a fit for you?"

- Or -

" _____, you probably get a lot of calls like these, so I'll be brief. I'll just ask you a couple of quick questions and if I think we can save you between 15 to 20% I'll let you know and, if not, we'll part friends, is that OK?"

4. Make a connection. This is one of the easiest of all and it's a great way to get your prospect talking. All you do is find something that you know is affecting your other clients (like new laws in their industry), and ask how it's affecting your new prospect.

"You know _____, a lot of my clients have told me of the changes they are having to make because of (the new law/change in regulation, etc.). How is that affecting you?"

- Or -

" _____ what are you planning to feature at the September trade show?"

By addressing something that they are dealing with now, you can instantly make a connection and get valuable information. *Warning*: you have to fit this in after you've established rapport, and you have to address something that is relevant to them.

5. Listen more. This may not seem like a way to sound natural on the phone, but believe me, it is the most important technique of all. Because most sales reps are so busy talking *at* their prospects, they lose them at the very beginning. In most cases, the prospect just turns off and waits for a pause where they can ditch the call.

By listening, you actually create space for your prospect to speak (and to think), and because of that you are allowing the conversation to flow. When you give the prospect a chance to get their thoughts and feedback out, they feel comfortable with you, and that is the best way for the conversation to unfold naturally. Hit your mute button after you ask a question and count three 1000's if you are having trouble remaining quiet.

There you have it - five easy ways to sound more natural on the phone. The good news is that they are easy to implement, and, once you do, you'll make more connections and you'll feel more comfortable on the phone. This will come across to your prospects and you'll end up qualifying better leads and making more sales.

2 | Overcoming Initial Resistance

How to Eliminate Screening Forever!

Dealing with gatekeepers is one of the most difficult and uncomfortable tasks in sales. Many salespeople make it worse on themselves because they try to manipulate or lie their way through to the decision maker. This never works and only alerts the gatekeeper that you are just another pesky sales rep.

How happy would you be to learn a proven technique that would get you past the gatekeeper almost 90% of the time? I know that is a big claim, but I guarantee that if you use the following techniques, your entire experience of cold calling will change, and gatekeepers will gladly put you through. They'll even be polite about it!

Three Techniques to Get Through Gatekeepers

Gatekeeper Technique #1 - Please Use Please: The single most powerful technique to get through gate keepers is the **Please use Please Technique.** Here's how you do it. Start your call with:

"Hi, could you please connect me with_____, please?"

Remember, it's a gatekeeper's job to SCREEN YOU OUT! So when they ask:

"Can I tell them who is calling?"

You respond with:

"Yes, please, please tell him _____ _____ with the (your company) is holding please." (Use please three times!)

Now please don't be fooled by how simple this seems. It will change your life on the phone, and you can demonstrate the incredible effectiveness of this technique by committing to using it today while making out-bound calls. I promise you will be amazed by your results.

Gatekeeper Technique #2 - Give Your Name and Company: Always give your complete name and company name – even if it doesn't mean anything to the gatekeeper. This is because:

- 80% of your competition is trying to dodge or trick the gatekeeper. This only encourages more screening!
- Giving both your first and last name and company name eliminates the need for further screening.

Gatekeeper Technique #3 - Use Instructional Statements: A primary function of a receptionist or secretary is to take instruction. Throughout their day they are directed to take care of many different tasks, and because of this they are used to taking and carrying out instructions. Because of this you should always end with an instructional statement. Here are examples of Instructional Statements:

Receptionist: "Can I tell him who is calling?"

You: "Yes, please, please tell him _____ _____ with the (your company) is holding please."

Receptionist: "Can I tell him what this is about?"

You: "Yes, please tell him it's about (the problem your prospect is having or your solution), please. I'll be happy to hold while you put me through."

I realize these gatekeeper techniques seem simple (and they are), but they are effective. Using these techniques, you will easily breeze past gatekeepers and screeners. Every salesperson who has used these techniques tells me the same thing – they not only work, but they eliminate 90% of screening they used to get. I guarantee that when you try them, you'll be saying the same thing as well.

How to Instantly Overcome Sales Resistance

Decision makers these days are busier than ever. They get lots of solicitations, and either don't have the time or don't want to take the time to field your call.

The mistake 80% of your competition make is they launch into their presentations trying to cram in their pitches, afraid that if they don't bulldoze ahead then they'll get blown off with a "no." You can imagine how that approach goes.

Others, aware of this problem, will politely ask "Is this is a good time?" Or, "Have I caught you in the middle of something?" Or, "Do you have a moment now?" While I understand being polite and accommodating, this approach usually just gives your prospects the easy way out. They get to say no without being rude, and you get nowhere.

Want a better way? Start by acknowledging in advance what you already know - they are busy. Then begin your presentation with a sentence or two, pausing briefly to take your prospect's pulse.

"Hi _____, this is _____ _____ with (your company) -- look I know you're busy so I'll keep this brief..."

- Or, if you sense they are ticked off or on guard -

"You know _____, I'm sure you get a lot of these kinds of calls don't you? I know, and believe me I don't like making them anymore than you like getting them. But every now and then something really good comes along and this is that day for you..."

- Or -

"I know you've probably got a lot going on right now, so I'll just ask you one quick question to see if this would make sense for you..." **(Make it an open-ended question!)**

These approaches work because they allow you to connect with and acknowledge where your prospect is in terms of their time and schedule, and yet still keep the conversation flowing.

Dealing With Initial Resistance

Eighty percent of sales reps who actually do get through to their prospects get blown out by the same old resistance that prospects have been using for years. Things like, "We already have a supplier" or "We don't have the budget" have been frustrating sales reps since the beginning of time.

Top 20% producers get these initial objections as well, but they easily handle them because they are prepared in advance with scripts that work. In addition to using proven scripts, they also understand the one secret to handling initial resistance:

Don't try to answer or overcome this initial resistance!

Instead, all you want to do is acknowledge you heard it, and then quickly move into your value statement and qualifying questions. Again, what's important here is that you don't go on the defensive and try to answer your prospect's initial resistance, and you don't go on the offensive either by challenging it or arguing with them.

All you want to do is acknowledge that you heard it, that you understand why your prospect might feel that way, and then move past it and into your brief presentation and qualifying questions. In many cases you may get another negative response from your prospect after trying to sidestep their first one. What you should do in this case is try another rebuttal here and ask another qualifying or opening question.

If you still get a "no" or "not interested," then be prepared to move on. Remember, most people you speak with *aren't going to be interested or qualified,* and your real job isn't filling your pipeline with unqualified prospects, but rather, finding qualified and interested buyers. Being prepared with and using the following scripts will allow you to overcome initial resistance, but when it turns out to be a real objection (like they really aren't interested or don't have the budget), then you get to thank them for their time and make another call to find someone who is interested and qualified.

And that's what using the following scripts will allow you to do. Remember – adjust, adapt, and rewrite these scripts to fit your product or service, and then be prepared to use them each and every time you get these initial objections. The most common reflex (initial resistance) responses you will get are:

- I'm not interested.
- Just send your information.
- We're already taken care of.
- I'm too busy, don't have the time.
- We don't have the money/budget.

Six "I'm not interested" Scripts

Your goal when dealing with *I'm not interested* is to earn the right to present your product or service. The following scripts are designed to help you sidestep this common reflex response and get on with your call objective.

I'm Not Interested - Response #1:

"That's fine _____, and many people I speak with tell me the same thing as well. But as they learn more about this and see what this can really do for them, they were glad they took a few minutes. One thing that would be a good fit for you is...." (Give a quick benefit, and then ask a qualifying question like, "Do you see how that would work for you?")

I'm Not Interested - Response #2:

"I didn't expect you to be interested _____, you don't know enough about this yet. But like me and everyone else, I do know you're interested in (provide a benefit here – saving money, increasing production, return, etc.) and that's why I'm calling. Let me ask you a quick question: If I could show you how you can (provide your unique benefit here) and even save you (time, money, etc.) wouldn't you be happy you took a few minutes to find out how?"

I'm Not Interested - Response #3:

"I know that _____, heck if you were interested you'd have called me! (Say this with a smile in your voice.) But seriously, I know you get a lot of calls, and every now and then it makes sense to listen to the right call, and this is it." (Continue on with your value proposition and then ask a question like, "Do you think that would help you, too?")

I'm Not Interested - Response #4:

"_____, you probably get a lot of these calls, don't you? You know, I get them, too, and believe me, I don't like getting them any more than you do. But every now and then I listen because sometimes there is information out there that will benefit me. And this is that kind of call for you. Let me ask you a quick question . . . " (Ask how they would like to improve, save, make more money using your product or service.)

I'm Not Interested - Response #5:

"Believe me, I'm with you. But the good news is that taking just 30 seconds with me right now could change the way you do business, and could help you (achieve your quotas, save thousands of dollars – whatever your product or service will do for them). In fact, let me share briefly with you how we've helped hundreds of companies just like yours..."

I'm Not Interested - Response #6:

"That's no problem, _____. I have a drawer full of clients who told me the same thing when I first called them as well. In fact, I'll put you in touch with some of them if you want. But the point is this: if you're like most people I speak with, you're having trouble (list the problems your product or service solves) and in a couple of minutes I can share with you the solutions to those problems that my other clients are enjoying right now. Let me ask you – If I can show you how you can (give benefit here), wouldn't it be worth a few minutes to find out how?"

Nine "Just send/fax/email the information (and I'll keep it on file/have a look at it, etc.)" Scripts

This is a standard blow off, and you must not make the mistake of just sending out your information. Remember, you're not in the brochure business! Use trial closes here to assess their level of interest:

Just Send Information - Response #1:

"I'll be happy to do that _____, but until we know if this is truly a fit for you, we'd be wasting your time. If you're serious about learning how this can actually help you, then I'd suggest we take a couple of minutes right now to discuss your situation. After that, if you're really interested I'd be glad to get something out to you – is that fair?"

Just Send Information - Response #2:

"I'd be happy to _____. Quick question though and please be honest with me: When do you think you'll be serious about moving on something like this?"

Just Send Information - Response #3:

"If you like what you see, when would you be ready to place an order?" Or, "Sure, and after you review it, how soon are you looking to make a decision on it?"

Just Send Information - Response #4:

"Before I do, I want to make sure you'd be ready to act on it if you like it. Let me ask you a quick question..." (Ask qualifying questions on budget, decision-making process, etc.)

Just Send Information - Response #5:

"_____, my experience is that information like this, even when it's this good, usually just gets buried under a stack of paper and that doesn't do either one of us any good. Now that we're on the phone together, I can answer any of your immediate questions and then you'll be in a better position to decide whether or not it makes sense to send you information. Let me ask you about your needs for this type of (your service or product)."

Just Send Information - Response #6:

"Absolutely. By the way, what would you need to see to say yes to it?"

Just Send Information - Response #7:

"You know _____, I get a lot of calls and when I'm really not interested, I tell the reps to just send their information and then I hope they lose my number. Be honest with me, is that what's happening here?"

Just Send Information - Response #8:

"I'll be happy to get this out to you in the next hour, but while I have you on the phone, let's first see if this can actually help you and if there's a real need on your end for this. How are you currently doing (ask about a process related to your product or service). And if I could show you how to (explain how your benefit would help them), would you seriously be willing to consider using our solution to help you?"

Just Send Information - Response #9:

"_____, let's be realistic here. I can send you all the information in the world, but if you're not ready or able to take advantage of it then we're just wasting each other's time. Now I'm happy to send you some information that will help you (state your unique benefit here), but let's have a quick discussion to see if this is something you'll actually move on. Now let me ask you..."

Twelve "We're happy/already taken care of/have a supplier/all set, etc." Scripts

This may be a real objection, but you must realize that THINGS CHANGE! Your goal here is to get them to think of you when they do. Here is the best script you can use to overcome this initial blow-off and set yourself up to be called back when things do change.

We're Happy - Response #1:

"I'm glad you're taken care of right now _____, and let me ask you something. If you ever found it necessary to get another (quote, point of view, find another vendor, information, etc.), could I be the first one in line to talk to you about some of your needs?"

- If yes -

"Great. I'll go ahead and send you some of my contact information; do me a favor and keep it with your (similar) records so you'll have it handy when you need some help with (your product or service)."

- Get all their contact information, then ask -

"Great. Just out of curiosity, _____ , what might have to happen for you to even consider looking at someone different?" (Qualify and expand on their answers here.)

We're Happy - Response #2:

"That's great _____, it tells me you understand the value of (or appreciate the benefits of) a (your product or solution). In fact, you're exactly the kind of company we work with. You see, I'm not suggesting you stop using what's working for you, but rather I'm here to help you get even better. You see the companies that use us have found that they can increase their (pitch your benefits here) by X%... And to see if this will work for you as well, let me just ask you a couple of quick questions." (Qualify for interest, control, and budget).

We're Happy - Response #3:

"_____ , when was the last time you took the time to do a serious 'apples to apples' comparison with another provider? Would you be open to finding out how we have helped other companies like yours and how we can perhaps make your job easier as well?"

We're Happy - Response #4:

"_____, I'm with you and let's face it, you're only going to switch providers if you're convinced you can find a better deal with better service. And you're going to need proof of that, aren't you? Well if I can provide that for you, would you at least be open to seriously considering it?"

We're Happy - Response #5:

"I understand, _____. And isn't it true that if you could get the same or even better results for less than you're spending right now, it'd be silly not to at least listen to how that might happen? You see, many of the clients I work with now told me the same thing but were happy they found out about our (introductory package, new client special, side by side comparison, etc.)"

We're Happy - Response #6:

"I know you have another company working with you and that's exactly why I'm calling you! The best thing about trying our service out is that you don't have to quit using who you are now, but rather, you get to try us out side by side and then make the best decision for you. I mean let me ask you – if you found a way to get better (service, results) for less money and still get better service, wouldn't you want to at least know about it?"

We're Happy - Response #7:

"_____, I'm not suggesting you discontinue using your current company for this, but rather, that you use us to compare the value you're currently getting now. Many of my clients found that they were able to reinforce their marketing message using our service and they were even able to double the amount of response from diverting just a portion of what they are currently spending now. Let me ask you..."

We're Happy - Response #8:

"No problem, _____. But let me just give you a quick comparison of the features you'll get by using us. After a couple of minutes you'll be in a much better position to decide whether it makes sense to look further into our company. Is that fair?"

We're Happy - Response #9:

"I'm glad you're taken care of. Quick question: When was the last time you made a serious comparison between who you're using now and the new programs other companies can offer you that might be a little bit better to a whole lot better?"

We're Happy - Response #10:

"I understand, and _____, the only reason companies switch suppliers is because they can get a better deal or better service, right? And that's what I'm offering you today. Let me ask you, if I could (fill in your specific feature or benefit here) would you at least be open to hearing more about it?"

We're Happy - Response #11:

"I understand _____, and let's face it – if you could invest the exact same amount of time and money as you're doing now and get even more business, it'd be a no-brainer to at least look at it, wouldn't it? Then let's take a couple of minutes right now. Let me ask you..."

We're Happy - Response #12:

"I'm glad you're already using someone because that's exactly what my other clients told me as well. In fact, I can email you a list of all the companies we've worked with last year and show you, case by case, how they were just like you and now they're (saving money, making more money, etc.) because they gave us a try. Let me ask you, if I could prove that we can meet or beat what your current supplier is offering you, would you be at least open to considering how it can help you?"

Nine "I'm too busy/don't have the time." Scripts

I'm too busy -Response #1:

"I know that feeling; my desk is full of things I need to do, too. I'd be happy to schedule a time to call you back, but I don't want to bother you if you're really not interested. Let me ask you a quick question and be honest with me: If I could show you a (system/product/service) that is proven to (reduce your overhead, generate more sales, etc.), would it be worth it for you and I to talk for just five minutes to see how it could work for you?"

- If NO -

"No problem. Before I go, who else do you know that might be able to use a system like this?"

- If Yes -

"Terrific. Do you have five minutes right now?"

- If No -

"I'm looking at my schedule. What is a good time later today?"

I'm too busy -Response #2:

"_____, you probably get a lot of calls like I do, and my initial reaction is to say I'm too busy as well. But I can explain this to you in just three minutes and if you think it can help you, we can schedule more time later. If you don't, we can part friends. Is that fair?"

I'm too busy -Response #3:

"I'm with you. Before I schedule time to get back with you, just a quick question: Is it a priority for you to (fix or improve what your product or service will do for them) this quarter?"

I'm too busy -Response #4::

"I'm glad you're busy – that means that you don't have the time to waste looking at things you have no intention of taking advantage of. Quick question: If I could show you a proven way to (get the benefits of your product or service), is that something that you would invest five minutes learning more about?"

I'm too busy -Response #5:

"No problem. I know what it's like to be interrupted. Would it be better to call you back right after your meeting, say in about a half hour, or would you prefer to set up a quick five minute call for tomorrow morning?"

I'm too busy -Response #6:

"Believe me I know what it's like to be busy! Do you have your calendar in front of you right now? Let's plan to talk later today or tomorrow morning - what works for you?"

I'm too busy -Response #7:

"I understand _____, but let's face it – we're never too busy to take two minutes to learn how to make more money with less effort and expense. Let me ask you one quick question: If I could show you a proven way to become more profitable and save money doing it, would you take a few minutes now to find out more?"

I'm too busy - Response #8:

"_____, many people ask me to describe this briefly and that almost never works. It just short-changes you. What I have is a proven system that has many customizable elements to fit your exact requirements and needs. What we provide isn't for everyone – it's an expensive solution but the return will pay you handsomely for many years to come. I can spend a couple of minutes with you now asking a couple of questions to see if this would fit, and, if it does, then we can schedule time to go over it in detail – is that fair?"

I'm too busy - Response #9:

"I understand and let me just ask you: You do see the value in a system like this, don't you?"

- If No -

"That's exactly why we need to spend more time together – you don't fully understand this yet. I've got some time tomorrow, what works for you?"

- If Yes -

"Good. Then let's go ahead and get some of your requirements right now, and I'll put together a starter program and you can be using this by the end of this week..."

Sixteen "We don't have the budget/money." Scripts

On the price objection it's especially important to remember that your goal here is not to overcome this, or find out if they really have the money or not, or help them to find the budget – that is your job during the close. Rather, your job here is to simply acknowledge this initial resistance and move past it and earn the right to deliver your pitch and qualify.

We don't have the budget - Response #1:

"Of course you don't have the money for something you know nothing about – that's why I'm calling you. Tell you what, let's take two to three minutes right now, and if you think this is something that will actually help you make more money (or get you more business, etc.), then we can see how it might fit in with you. Let me ask you..."

We don't have the budget - Response #2:

"That's exactly why I'm calling! You see, if you were already using us then you'd have a lot more sales and revenue and money wouldn't be an issue. I find that the companies who tell me they can't afford it actually need it the most. Let's do this, I'll ask you a couple of quick questions to see if this can help you and if we should continue from there – fair enough?"

We don't have the budget - Response #3:

"_____, not many companies/people I call have money lying around waiting for my call. Rather, like you, they have their money invested in other places working for them. All I want to do for you now is help you see if there are better places for your money to work for you – and if there are, wouldn't it at least make sense to consider moving some resources around to take advantage of them?"

We don't have the budget - Response #4:

"I totally understand that _____, but let's put the money aside for a moment and see if this is even a fit for you first. If it's not, then it doesn't matter whether you have the money or not, and if it is, then I'm sure you can find the money. Now let me ask you…"

We don't have the budget - Response #5:

"_____, we can all find the funds for something if it makes sense. Let's do the smart thing and talk about whether this could actually help you – that doesn't cost anything! And then if it makes sense, we'll work on finding the money for it later. Let me ask you, how are you currently handling your…"

We don't have the budget - Response #6:

"Where do you usually get budget from when you find something that you absolutely must have?"

We don't have the budget - Response #7:

"_____, it's much too early to talk about money, and I wouldn't expect you to be ready to buy something you know nothing about. Let's do this: I'll spend just a couple of minutes with you to see if this would work for you in your environment and, if it makes sense, then we can talk about how we would integrate it. Does that make sense?"

We don't have the budget - Response #8:

"_____, none of us have money for something we don't understand – and that's what this call is about. You see, I'm not calling to have you spend money with me today. Rather, I'm calling to see if I can help you (achieve your financial goals, increase sales, make more money, etc.). And if I can, then we can talk about the best way to proceed. Now, let me ask you a couple of quick questions to see if it makes sense for us to work together..."

We don't have the budget - Response #9:

"_____, if I could show you a way to save 10 to 15% each year on your current operating costs, and I could prove it to you, do you think it would be worth it to find the money somewhere?"

We don't have the budget - Response #10:

"You know I admit our solution isn't cheap, however, the best things in life never are. But the good news is that (top companies, financial advisors, business people like you) have looked very carefully into (our product or solution) and they have compared it to all the other solutions on the market and they decided to spend the money and go with us. Let me tell you the top three reasons why they did that..."

We don't have the budget - Response #11:

"No problem _____, and the good news is that there is no charge now to listen. Here's what I'll do for you – I'll simply ask you a couple of questions right now to see which of our programs might make your job a lot easier, and if you agree, then we can talk about the investment. Now, let me ask you how you're currently..."

We don't have the budget - Response #12:

"And that's exactly why we offer our low-cost, introductory package. You see _____, we know that once you see how much more business this brings you, you'll come to see this as an investment, not an expense. And if this works for you like it does our other clients, improving their results by 12% on average, what kind of increase in sales and revenue would that mean to you?"

We don't have the budget - Response #13:

"_____, I know that if you gave me $500 today and I gave you back $2,000 over the course of the next six months, then you'd find the money in about five minutes, wouldn't you? All I'm saying is that my solution might work like this for you, and it'll only take a few minutes to find that out if it would. That's worth a few minutes of your time, isn't it?"

We don't have the budget - Response #14:

"The good news is that this will actually save you money, so cost is never a problem because it pays for itself. The real issue is whether or not you're a candidate for it. Let me ask you a couple of quick questions to see..."

We don't have the budget - Response #15:

"_____, if you don't have the money now, then you actually need this more than most people I speak with. You see, the value you'll get by using this system will actually save you money and make you money so you'll never again have to live with the sick feeling that you never have any money. Are you ready to make that change in your life?"

We don't have the budget - Response #16:

"_____, we can all find the money when we really need to. I mean, if your car broke down on the way home, you'd gladly pay $500, $1,000 or more to have it working again by tomorrow, wouldn't you? You'd put it on a credit card and pay it off each month, wouldn't you? Then do yourself a favor and be open to using your business credit card for this as well, and as it begins to save and even make you money, you'll be ahead of the game in the long run. That's called making a wise investment. Now, let me ask you..."

This concludes the section on handling initial resistance. As you can see, all of these rebuttals have the same thing in common – they don't try to answer or overcome the objections, rather, they simply acknowledge them and allow you to move on to your presentation and qualify your prospect. This is crucial to understand.

You can use these as templates for almost any initial resistance statement you get. Once you've found your favorites, use them over and over again until they become your own reflex responses to the ones you hear from your prospects and clients. Adapt them to fit your product or service.

You'll find more price rebuttals in the "Overcoming Objections" section later on. It is during the close that you actually have to handle the price objection, and that section is filled with proven, ready-to-use scripts to help you do just that.

3 | Top 20% Techniques For Dealing With Difficult Prospects

The mark of Top 20% producers is the ability to effectively deal with difficult prospects and situations. Handling negative prospects, disqualifying non-buyers and knowing how to isolate potential objections in advance are skills that separate the Top 20% from their competition.

What the Top 20% know is most selling situations and potential problem areas are the same time and again. Their advantage is *preparation*. Top 20% sales professionals prepare in advance with proven and effective ways to deal with difficult situations. This section will provide you with the scripts, techniques and skills you'll need to anticipate and successfully deal with the obstacles and situations that frustrate the bottom 80%.

Five Ways to Handle the "No Budget" Objection in a Tough Economy

It's no surprise that the biggest objection you will face in a tough economy is the "no budget" objection. Now, does this mean that companies aren't buying anything? Of course not! Think about your own life – when times are tough you're still shopping, buying, and getting ready for vacations and holidays, aren't you? You are just being a little more cautious.

So are your prospects. They are still buying things (like your product or solution), but they are being just a bit more cautious. This means you have to be more creative with how you handle the initial resistance of no budget. Here are five proven ways of dealing with no budget:

No Budget Response #1:

"I understand and I'm not calling to sell you anything today - that's not what this call is about. I'm simply calling to see if my company is a fit for what you're doing over there, and if we are, then to provide you with our information as a resource for the future when you do have the budget. Now let me ask you..."

(Start a dialogue and ask qualifying questions to see how you can help them, and watch their resistance come down and their buying signals come out!)

No Budget Response #2:

"_____, that's exactly why I'm calling you. You see we work with (their kind of company) all the time and our solution actually saves you money. That's why so many companies invest a portion of their budgets into our (your product or service). But before we even talk about that, it's important to see if this can help you, too. I just have a couple of quick questions...." (ask a key qualifying question now.)

No Budget Response #3:

"I know exactly what you mean, things are tough all over. Let me ask you this: Where do you normally get the budget from when an unexpected expense comes up?"

No Budget Response #4:

"That's perfectly OK. I don't expect you to even consider spending money on something you know nothing about, and that's why I'm here. Let me ask you a couple of quick questions, and if there is a fit between our companies, then you can determine if it makes sense to learn more about how our (your product or service) can help you (save money, make more money, save time which is money, etc.). Now…"

No Budget Response #5:

"_____, if you're like most of my clients right now you're going to be extremely cautious regarding any money you spend, so I totally understand. Let's not talk about budget until we determine if our (your product or service) even makes sense for you. Let me ask you this…" (ask a qualifying question to determine if it makes sense to keep talking to them)

Seven Scripts For Dealing With Negative Prospects

Invariably while cold calling, you will run up against a prospect who just doesn't want to listen to anything you have to say. The key is getting them to open up. If you run into a prospect that doesn't believe in what your product can do, you should respond:

Negative Prospect Script #1:

"_____, I know you get a lot of calls like these and I'm sure it gets tiring to hear the same old claim over and over. But the truth is, this is the one call this month that is worth your taking five minutes to participate in. Let me ask you…" (ask a good, benefits-filled qualifying question here).

Negative Prospect Script #2:

"_____, just imagine for a moment that what I was saying did work out and you were already a client enjoying the steady monthly income, what would you be thinking now?"

Negative Prospect Script #3:

"Just suppose for a moment that my product was able to reduce the time and money you now spend in this area just like it does for my other clients. Wouldn't you be happy you took a few minutes now to discuss this?"

Negative Prospect Script #4:

"_____, no good idea ever entered a closed mind. Now you didn't get to your position by saying no to everything. Rather, you probably had the good sense to be open-minded and to evaluate new ideas based on what they had to offer. Let's do this – let's take just two minutes to find out if this can help you, and if it can, we'll schedule time later to go through it. Isn't that fair?"

Negative Prospect Script #5:

"_____, as a (their position), you probably get pitched all the time, so I don't blame you for being gruff with me right now. But let's be honest – every now and then you have to be open to new ideas that will help you, and I've got one right now. Let's make a deal: I'll ask you a couple of quick questions and if it makes sense for you to hear more, we'll schedule a time for me to (call you back or visit with you) and you can learn more. Now, let me ask you..."

Negative Prospect Script #6:

"_____, why do you think that some of the (top business people, top financial advisors, your top business competitors), are recommending or participating in this very same (program or product) right now?"

Negative Prospect Script #7:

"_____, I don't blame you for being negative right now. I hate it too when sales reps call me and try to sell me something. Tell you what I'll do. I'll put something in writing to you and you can review it at your leisure – will that work? Great. Then let me ask you briefly how you're currently handling . . ." (qualify here and try to open up the dialogue).

These are great techniques to get your prospect thinking positively about reasons why they should buy from you.

Eight Scripts For Dealing With Difficult Put-offs

Many times prospects truly have no interest but they either don't know how or won't come out and tell us. Instead they will say things like, "Go ahead and send me the (information, brochure, demo) and I'll take a look." Or, "Put that quote in writing and send it to me."

When a Top 20% closer hears this, his/her first thought is, "I don't have the time to do that, and I especially don't have the time to follow up with an unqualified lead." Here's how they handle it and how you should, too:

Go ahead and send me your information - Script #1:

"I'd be happy to, and if you like what you see would you be ready to place an order?"

Go ahead and send me your information - Script #2:

"Before I do, I want to make sure you'd be ready to act on it if you like it. Let me briefly ask you..." (Ask qualifying questions on budget, decision-making process, etc.)

Go ahead and send me your information - Script #3:

"Sure, and after you review it, how soon are you going to make a decision on it?"

Go ahead and send me your information - Script #4:

"Sure. And what would you need to see to say yes to it?"

-Or-

Put that quote in writing and send it to me - Script #1

"I'd be happy to, and from what we've just discussed, does it sound like you'd go with it?"

Put that quote in writing and send it to me - Script #2

"Absolutely. How does this compare with the other quotes you've received so far?"

Put that quote in writing and send it to me - Script #3

"Great. Based on the quote/price I just gave you does this sound like it fits into your budget?"

Put that quote in writing and send it to me - Script #4

"I'd be happy to, and after you get it, what happens next?"

Bottom line - the Top 20% don't have time for the put-off game, and you shouldn't either.

How to Handle the Price Question:

When a prospect asks you about the price of your product or service, Top 20% closers know that what's important is not that you tell them (which is fine), but rather what happens next. After answering the price question, most salespeople either:

• Remain silent, waiting for the prospect to ask another question.

• Start pitching and justifying the price of their product or service.

• Move on to another qualifying question.

Guess what? All these responses are wrong. If you do any of these things, you are missing a golden opportunity to find out where your prospect stands in regards to budget. What is the right question? Ask them how they feel or where they stand in regards to the price you just gave them. Use any of these questions:

• How does that price sound to you?

• Is that within your budget?

• Which of those price points appeal to you the most?

• Is that what you are looking to spend?

Whenever your prospect asks about the price, and you give it, you must qualify on it. The Top 20% automatically do this and move that much closer to getting the information they need to make a sale.

Scripts For Dealing With Difficult Assistants

One of the biggest mistakes salespeople make is treating personal assistants, office managers, and other people standing between them and the decision maker the same as they treat gatekeepers.

An assistant is not a receptionist, and you must know the difference. A receptionist or true gatekeeper is someone who takes and screens incoming calls. An assistant, on the other hand, is someone who works closely with your prospect, has keen insights into what they may or may not like or need, and often has influence on whether or not you get to the decision maker - and how you will be received once you do.

Most salespeople simply try to get around assistants, but the Top 20% treat them with respect. In doing so, they gain valuable information. One of the best ways to deal with assistants is to use the "Perhaps you can help me" technique. Remember, your goal is to get information that will help you be more prepared for dealing with the decision maker. Start by first acknowledging assistants with:

Assistant: "_____ isn't here right now, can I take a message?"

Rep: "I'm glad I reached you. Perhaps you can help me first. You probably work pretty closely with _____ don't you?"

- If yes, say -

"That's great. Let me ask you, how is he/she handling (your product area)?"

Start your qualifying questions now. Find out information like:

• Who are they using now?

• How does the decision process work?

- What does the decision maker like/dislike?

- When are they making a decision on this?

- What's important to them?

- When is the best time to reach them?

When you reach an office manager or an assistant, be glad you did. You will have the opportunity to get additional information that can often give you the competitive edge. Once you get in the habit of treating assistants with the respect they deserve, you'll be amazed at how they will help you.

How to Handle Incoming Leads

Many salespeople believe that just because a prospect has called in, that they are more qualified. But this isn't necessarily true. In fact, this belief leads to the biggest mistake salespeople make when dealing with warm leads - they go into pitch mode rather than qualification mode. They mistake the "implied interest" of a call-in lead to mean they are already qualified, and all they need to do is explain their product or service. Wrong!

The Top 20%, on the other hand, know that warm leads can be among the biggest time wasters in sales. With warm leads they do what they always do – they disqualify people who are "just look-ing" so they can spend their valuable time with real buyers. With warm leads, they ask questions rather than pitch. Here are qualifi-cation questions to ask the next time you get a warm lead:

Warm Lead Qualifying Question #1:

"Thank you for contacting us. What was it about our ad/promotion/ website that caused you to call us today?" (Listen for the buying motive.)

Warm Lead Qualifying Question #2:

"Who else are you looking into?" (Listen for your competition.)

Warm Lead Qualifying Question #3:

"What do you like best so far?" (Listen for why they might not choose you.)

Warm Lead Qualifying Question #4:

"How long have you been thinking about (buying, investing, changing) something like this?"

- Then -

"What has kept you from acting on this?" (Listen for their objection.)

Warm Lead Qualifying Question #5:

"What other kinds of quotes have you gotten on this?"

- Then -

"And why haven't you moved forward with them?"

- Or -

"When are you looking to make a decision on this?"

Warm Lead Qualifying Question #6:

"When are you looking to make a purchase on this?"

Warm Lead Qualifying Question #7:

"If I could help you find what you need, are you thinking about buying/purchasing/investing today?"

Warm Lead Qualifying Question #8:

"What is the one thing that attracted you to our website/ company/ product?"

Warm Lead Qualifying Question #9:

"I'm glad you called on that because we still have some in stock. How many are you looking for today?"

Warm Lead Qualifying Question #10:

"Tell me a little about what you're looking for in a (company, product, service) like ours?"

Warm Lead Qualifying Question #11:

"Thank you for sharing that with me. The good news is that I can get that for you today and we're offering a 10% discount for all orders placed today only. Where would you like that shipped to?"

Warm Lead Qualifying Question #12:

"I'd be happy to look that up for you Are you looking to place an order on that today?"

Warm Lead Qualifying Question #13:

"What would you need to see to decide to move forward with this?"

Just remember, to be a Top 20% producer, you have to begin finding buyers -- whatever the lead source. So stop pitching and start qualifying!

The Most Important Button on Your Phone

Have you ever needed to ask directions? You know, you're traveling and trying to get to your hotel, or on the other side of town looking for a restaurant. You are lost so you stop and ask someone for direction.

When the other person starts giving you directions, what do you do? You listen, don't you? The person who is speaking has the information you need to get where you are going. If you don't listen you will remain lost. You take mental notes and ask clarifying questions when you don't fully understand something.

Compare this type of attentive listening with the listening that most salespeople do while on the phone with prospects. 80% of the reps I observe are pitching more than listening, and they're jumping in as soon as their prospect takes a breath. Most of the time, they aren't really hearing what their prospect is saying. Rather, they are just waiting for their turn to talk.

Given this lack of listening and questioning, it's not hard to understand why most salespeople struggle to make sales.

Listening is the number one skill of Top 20% producers. They are successful listeners because they actually hear what is behind what their prospects are saying, and they know how to ask clarifying questions to get them to reveal even more.

So, how can you get better at listening? Simple: Use the most important button on your phone – the MUTE button! Here's how:

Whenever you ask your prospect a question, hit your mute button. While this may be uncomfortable at first, you will get four key benefits from using your mute button:

1.   It will force you to stop talking over your prospect. You'll still be able to blurt stuff out, but your prospect won't hear it.

2.   The silence on your end will also encourage your prospect to keep talking and as they do, they'll reveal crucial information you can use to close them – if you just let them.

3.   By remaining silent, your prospect will literally "feel heard," and this will help you build a stronger feeling of rapport – which will get them talking even more.

4.   By learning to really listen, you will finally get comfortable with the sales process and begin to tell who's likely to be a real deal and who's not. Listening for and hearing this difference is the true mark of a top closer.

There are many more benefits to using your mute button, and I'll let you discover them on your own. Ultimately, when you listen as if you are *lost,* you will find that your prospects give you the exact directions to close them.

Voicemail Scripts

I don't know about you, but I'm shocked every time I listen to a voicemail message left for me by sales reps, prospects and even clients. They are filled with 'um's' and 'ah's', they ramble on and on, they leave no compelling reason for me to call back, and they almost always leave their number so fast that I have to listen to it two, three, sometimes four times to make it out! It's no wonder so many voicemail messages get deleted and never called back!

If ever there was a situation that begged to be scripted, it's your voicemail message. Isn't this the time you want to sound your best, be perceived as a professional, and prepare the most polished message you can? Of course it is. Here are seven voicemail messages that will separate yours from the other 80% of voicemails that get ignored, deleted and never returned.

The first two voicemail scripts are for prospects you haven't spoken with previously, and the next three are for calling a prospect or client back. The final two are for situations when your prospect or client isn't calling you back.

Voicemail scripts for prospects you haven't spoken with previously

New Prospect Voicemail Script #1:

Note: The best voicemail message has a specific purpose that addresses the needs of your prospect or client, and offers them a solution that is worth them taking the time to call you back to learn more about. Here is the classic template – adjust and adapt it to fit your product or service. In this and all examples, leave your phone number SLOWLY:

"Hi _____, this is _____ with (your company). I'm calling about your new office that's opening in Houston next month, and I wanted to provide you with some ideas that may help with your networking issues. We work with a lot of companies in the area, and I think you'll find it useful if we talk. You can reach me by calling area code (your number). That number again is (your number), and ask for _____. I look forward to speaking with you, and thanks in advance for returning my call."

New Prospect Voicemail Script #2:

"Hi _____, this is _____ _____ with (your company). You and I haven't spoken yet, but I've been doing some research on your company and I think you're a great fit for (our networking solutions – your products here). We can provide you with (brief list of one or two benefits) and I know you'll be happy if we spend just a couple of minutes discussing how this can help you. When you get this message, please call me back at (your number). That number again is (your number), and ask for _____. I look forward to speaking with you, and I guarantee you'll be glad you returned this call."

New Prospect Voicemail Script #3:

"Hi _____, this is _____ _____ with (your company). Briefly _____, I need to speak with you about how you're handling your sales tracking (Or your kind of product or service), because I have something that can (solve their unique problem). Our clients include (list some companies they are familiar with), and I know this would work for you as well. Believe me it'll be worth a five minute phone call to find out why. Please do me a favor when you get this message and call me back at (your number). That number again is (your number), and ask for _____. I look forward to speaking with you and I promise you'll be glad you returned this call."

Follow-up voicemails left for prospects (or clients)

Follow-up Voicemail Script #1:

"Hi _____, this is _____ _____ with (your company) getting back with you. I'm looking forward to speaking with you because we just (give an update here – you have a new special, new product update, added a new client they would know about), and I know that based on (their specific need you uncovered during the last call) this is going to make it even easier for you to (give the benefit you both discussed). I'm excited to share this with you. Do me a favor when you get this message and please give me a call back at (your number). That number again is (your number). I look forward to speaking with you."

Follow-up Voicemail Script #2:

"Hi _____, this is _____ _____ getting back with you about (your demo, quote, etc.). Briefly, I've been doing some more research on how we may be able to save you even more (or make you even more – whatever your product or service can do for them), especially in regards to your (list a specific need they told you about during the initial call), and I'm excited to share that (or discuss that) with you. I'll be in my office the rest of today, so do me a favor when you get this message and please give me a call back at (your number). That number again is (your number). I look forward to speaking with you."

Voicemails left for prospects who are dodging you or not calling you back

Get Back To Me Voicemail Script #1:

"Hi _____, this is _____ _____ again with (your company). For some reason we haven't been able to connect since I sent you (your demo, proposal, etc.), and believe me, I've been in sales long enough to know what that might mean. I'm assuming you've either found another solution or this has been put on the

back burner for now. Either way, that's fine.
Please do me a favor though. So I'm not bothering you anymore, could you please give me a quick call and just give me an update so I know what direction you're moving in? If I'm not available, just leave me a voicemail. Again, either way, it will be good to know what's going on.

Thanks in advance for that and I'll look for your call. You can reach me at (your number). That number again is (your number). Thanks again, _____."

Get Back To Me Voicemail Script #2:

"Hi _____, this is _____ _____ again with (your company). I'm sorry we haven't been able to get back together on this – if you're like me, then I'm sure you're being pulled in many different directions and are real busy. Do me a favor, though, when you get this message just call me back and leave me a voicemail with what you've decided to do about (your proposal or demo or quote). If you're still interested in it, great, but even if you've decided not to move forward with it, that's fine as well. Either way it will be nice for me to know.

Thanks in advance for that, and I'll look for your call. You can reach me at (your number). That number again is (your number). Thanks again, _____."

There you have it – voicemail messages for most of the situations you'll find yourself in. Once again, by using these scripted, proven messages you'll be giving yourself the best chance to hear back from your prospects and clients. And remember, even if their answer is "no," that's a lot better than chasing unqualified prospects who are never going to buy.

Six Secrets For Winning E-mails

Across the board, e-mail open rates are going down. With so many e-mails hitting your prospects' inbox, few are actually read. Most are quickly deleted. What I've found, however, is that there are some techniques that can give you the best chance of getting your e-mails read and even responded to, but you have to be very specific in the way you construct them. Follow these six e-mail secrets to get more and better responses:

E-mail Secret #1: Use the prospect's first name in the subject line. Think about it. What is everyone's favorite word? Their first name! Have you ever been in public before and heard someone call out your name? You automatically turned around and were receptive and ready to respond until you saw they were calling to someone else they knew.

You can get your prospect's attention the same way by putting their name in the subject line of your e-mails. To start with, doing so will distinguish your e-mail from the hundreds of others your prospect receives, and because we are all drawn to our own name, it will draw your prospect's eyes to your email like a magnet. This is the very best way to get their attention, and a great way to get them to read more.

E-mail Secret #2: Customize the first few lines of your e-mail as much as possible. Many people preview their e-mails by reading the first few sentences in their e-mail program before deciding to read the whole thing, so concentrate on writing a short and value-laden opening that is addressed right to them. Something like:

"Hi Barbara, Mike Brooks here with HMS Software. I've got some ideas about your networking issues for your new office that's opening in Houston next month. I think you'll find it useful if we talk."

Again, keep it short, customize it to what you know they're interested in, and provide immediate, specific value to them.

E-mail Secret #3: Keep your e-mail short and easy to read. Nothing will turn your prospect off more than long, information-packed paragraphs. Their eyes will glaze over and they will hit the delete key faster than it took you to hit the send key!

Don't let any of your paragraphs be more than three sentences, and, if possible, make them just two sentences. Recap the major ideas in short phrases, and make sure to engage your prospect by asking questions. An example would be:

"Hi John, I was wondering if you were still having trouble recouping all the available cash from your current collection program? If so, you'll want to speak with me about our new itemized IT solution.

I've got some time next Tuesday or would later in the week work for you? Please let me know either way. You can see more info here: (your website address).

If I don't hear from you, I'll follow up with a call next week."

E-mail Secret #4: Ask for a return response – whether they are interested or not. This is a great way to end your e-mail and a good way to get a response. Just think about how nice it will be to finally take someone off your list who isn't going to do business with you, and also how great it will be to find someone who is!

Simply thank them in advance for their consideration and let them know that you're looking forward to their response on this – either a "yes" or a "no."

E-mail Secret #5: Promise to follow up by phone if they don't respond. Let them know that you understand they are busy, and that if you don't hear from them, then you'll follow up with a call in a day or two.

This really increases your response rate and you can be happy when you get a "not interested" response. These prospects just disqualified themselves and saved you a lot of time and energy!

On the other hand, there will be others who don't respond and they become your follow-up leads.

E-mail Secret #6: Proofread your e-mails before you hit the send key. Because your prospects can't see you, they only have your writing sample on which to judge you. If it is filled with misspellings and poor grammar, what kind of impression do you think this makes?

It only takes a minute to proofread your e-mails, and I'll tell you now I'm always glad I did. I almost always make them better, and when I hit the send key, I know I've sent out the best message possible. Doing so allows me to make the best impression, and this, once again, separates me from my competition.

4 | Qualifying

The Most Important Step In the Sales

Process

The number one reason salespeople don't close more business is because they are selling to unqualified leads. In their haste to "fill their pipelines," salespeople will generate a lead or set an appointment with just about anyone who seems interested, and waste their valuable time and energy chasing and pitching prospects who are never going to be a deal.

In the previous chapters, you learned how to deal with blow-off and put-off statements to separate non-interested prospects from those worth spending time with. In this chapter you will learn how to use specific questions and scripts to further qualify buyers.

Qualifying is critical! So much so, that very often, your closing ratio is a direct correlation to your effectiveness at qualifying prospects.

*The brutal reality is you can't close an
unqualified prospect.*

The good news is, if you qualify your prospects well, you will close more business in less time. However, if you don't, you will spend your days and weeks being drained of energy by prospects who will never buy.

The Five Elements of a Qualified Prospect

There are five things that every Top 20% producer knows when he or she hangs up the phone with a prospect.

If you know these five things, there is a high probability that you will close the deal. Miss one or two and chances are even better that you're never going to make the sale. It's as simple as that. Here are the five elements of a qualified prospect:

1. Decision maker and decision process. When speaking with your prospect, you need to be very clear on whether or not they are the sole decision maker, or if others are involved in the decision.

A great question to ask here is an assumptive question like:

"_____, besides yourself, who else is involved in the decision process here?"

- Or -

"_____, who do you run things by when making a decision like this?"

The power of asking an assumptive question here is that people almost always involve others when making a decision. Just asking _if_ they are the decision maker allows them to create a smokescreen. I'm sure you've gotten the "Well, I need to run this by _____" when you have attempted to close prospects who have told you that they are the decision maker. Use either of the two questions above to avoid that.

You also need to understand the decision process. What's involved? Who's in charge? Uncover this by asking questions like:

"After you review this, what happens next?"

- Or -

"And after you receive the information/demo/etc., what is the evaluation process like?"

If you are not absolutely clear on this when you get off the phone, then you don't have a qualified lead.

2. Time frame. Part of knowing who and how the decision is made also involves knowing the time frame for making the decision. You must be clear on when they need your product or service, what type of urgency there is (if any), and when they are making the final decision. Ask these questions:

"And when would you like to see a decision like this made?"

- Or -

"_____, assuming this is a fit for you, when is the board meeting to vote on this? And if they approve it, when are you planning to implement it?"

- Or -

"_____, to make sure we can accommodate this, what time frame are you looking at to get this rolling, assuming it's a go?"

3. Other quotes. You also need to know what other quotes, products, solutions, or options your prospect is considering. If they have a regular vendor and are getting other bids, you especially need to know:

• How many other bids are they are getting?

• Why are they looking for other bids? (Do they just need to get other bids before going with last year's vendor?)

- What are they looking for in another bid?

- What will make yours the one they choose?

Knowing about your competition is crucial and it's one of the things that most sales reps avoid asking about. They are afraid that it will "kill" the deal, but wouldn't you rather know about this up front?

4. Buying motives (needs and wants). It is crucial for you to have a clear understanding of what is truly motivating your prospect to buy. You must be able to answer these questions:

- What exactly is the prospect looking for?

- What are their unique buying motivations? Why are they looking? What's motivating them to act now?"

- What do you need to say to sell them? (Everybody has key words and phrases, and if you ask the right questions and truly listen, they will tell you. Do you know what they are when you get off the phone?)

5. Why they won't buy. Just as important as knowing why they will buy is knowing why they won't buy from you. When you hang up the phone you need to know:

- Why are they really getting another quote?

- What are some of their sore spots?

- What are they trying to avoid?

- Why won't they buy?

Try these questions:

"_____, I see you've looked at our solution before -- what kept you from moving forward with it?"

- Or -

"_____, while this may be a fit for you, what can you see that might come up to prevent you from going with this?"

- Or -

"How long have you been thinking about this? And what has kept you from acting on it?"

- Or -

"What's changed this time? And might that stop you again?"

These five elements are the bare minimum of what you need to know about every prospect you qualify. These points form the basis of your qualifying checklist, and you need to have scripted questions that you ask on each and every call to uncover this information. You will find more detailed checklists and qualifying questions in my book: *The Real Secrets of the Top 20% - How To Double Your Income Selling Over the Phone.*

The Disqualifying Question

I remember I was training a group of inside sales software reps in Northern California once and I asked the pivotal question:

"Out of every ten prospects, how many end up buying?"

While their answer was discouraging, it was by no means out of the norm: "One or two" they replied. Think about that – one or two prospects end up turning into deals. I hear this ratio (or something similar), from the thousands of sales reps I work with each year.

The awful thing is that so many salespeople spend much of their time chasing and pitching prospects that ARE NEVER GOING TO CLOSE! No wonder most reps leave work on Friday beaten down and dreading Monday.

It's not like that for the Top 20%, though. In fact, in that same group of software sales reps, there was a top producer who earned seven figures. His secret? If a prospect didn't answer eight or nine out of out ten specific questions, he didn't pursue the lead. Period.

If your sales philosophy is a numbers game, i.e., "If I send out enough paper (or qualify enough prospects) then somebody is likely to close." I urge you to change it. This philosophy is exhausting and ineffective.

So what is one thing you can do right now to instantly get out more qualified prospects? Ask what I call "The Disqualifying Question." It goes like this:

If while you are qualifying a prospect you are getting red flags, instead of going on, and on ask this question:

"_____, if I get this demo, info, etc., off to you, what do you think might/could happen that would stop you from moving ahead with it?"

Then shut up and listen. The answer you get here will be the same one your prospect will give you when you call back and lose the sale. The Top 20% would rather know this in advance and so they use this question all the time to disqualify out a non-buyer.

Important note -- I realize this is a negative question and one you would normally not ask. You use it only when your gut tells you there's going to be a problem here – like when you keep getting red flags. Make sense?

The problem for the bottom 80% is they ignore these red flags and subsequently waste their time with prospects who are never going to buy.

The Top 20% would rather know on the front end if there's going to be a problem, and really, wouldn't you? So, in addition to using a qualifying checklist, make sure to use The Disqualifying Question whenever you think there could be a problem. You will have fewer prospects in your pipeline, but your closing ratio will improve. And that means you'll make more money!

How to Deal With Red Flags

One of the biggest mistakes 80% of salespeople make when qualifying is to overlook or not react to obvious red flags prospects give them during the initial call. In their haste or desperation to fill their pipeline, most salespeople hope that the possible objection they just heard will miraculously go away once the prospect sees their information or product or service, etc.

It never does. What appears to be an objection or deal killer always is. Never, ever forget *The Golden Rule of Qualifying:*

LEADS NEVER GET BETTER

I remember one salesperson who told me about a prospect who wasn't calling him back only to find out the prospect was leaving the company. He told me, "I guess intuitively I knew he wasn't the right guy to make the decision anyway."

And I'll bet he knew that because he heard (but didn't question!) the red flags that came up during the initial qualification call.

So how do you deal with red flags? Do what the Top 20% do - as soon as you hear something that triggers your intuition or that gives you that sick feeling in your gut, stop and ask the tough questions! Here's how you do it:

1. **If your prospect says that they usually buy from _____, but would like to see your information, ask:**

"Why would you switch vendors?"

- Or -

"How many other companies have you looked at in the last six months?"

- And then -

"And how many did you go with?"

2. **If your prospect says that they will pass it on to _____, say:**

"Thanks. So that I make sure I'm not wasting her time, it's best that I speak with her for just a few minutes. Can you please tell her that (your name) is holding please?"

If you're then told they are not available, make sure and get their direct line or the person's extension and keep calling until they pick up.

3. If your prospect says that they'd be glad to look it over, ask:

"Great. After you do, if you think that it can help you (or your business, etc.) when would you be thinking of moving on it?"

- And then -

"And what has to happen in the meantime?"

- Or -

"And who gets involved in a decision like this?"

4. If your prospect says they don't have time to talk about it now but that you can send your information, say:

"I'd be happy to, but before we waste your valuable time, it's best we make sure this is a fit for you. Let's do this, I'll ask you a couple of quick questions to see if this is worth your time. If it is, I'd be happy to send it. Now...."

- Or -

"I understand you're busy. Quick question: If this (your solution) worked for you here, when are you and your team making a decision on it?"

- Or -

"No problem. Very quickly, is something like this a decision you're looking at making this (month, quarter, fiscal year)?"

The bottom line is that if you want to close like the Top 20%, then you have to start questioning the red flags.

Remember: It's better to disqualify the non-buyers early than to spend your time and energy chasing and pitching people who are never going to buy.

This week, write questions to the red flags you currently get and begin using them! You'll feel so much stronger as a closer, and you'll make more money.

The Power of Layering Questions

First, for those of you who have seen me live, you know that I am big on questioning your prospects during the qualification stage. As I've said, your prospects have all the answers as to why they will buy or will not buy, and it is your job to get them to reveal this to you.

While asking well thought out, scripted questions is certainly a good start, you will get the most thorough and complete information if you learn to use layering questions.

The reason layering questions are so valuable is they get your prospect to go deeper into an area of interest they have, or into an area of concern. By scripting out and using layering questions consistently, you will be able to fully understand what is driving your prospect to make a decision, and/or why your prospect might not be ready to do business with you.

Knowing this information will move you that much closer to getting the sale.

Here are some examples of layering questions for qualifying buyer motivation.

1. When qualifying to find out who is involved in the decision process, you're going to start with a nice assumptive question, like:

"Besides yourself, who else is involved in the decision process?"

- And when they say their spouse, manager, or boss, etc., you then layer the question by asking –

"And what do you think they would do?"

- Or -

"Which direction are they leaning in regards to this?"

- Or -

"What do they usually do in this kind of situation?"

2.   If your prospect is looking at other vendors:

"Tell me _____, who else are you looking at in regards to this solution?"

- And your layering questions -

"And which companies look good to you so far?"

- Or -

"Who are you leaning toward right now?"

- Or -

"If you had to make a decision today, who would you go with?"

- And then ask -

"Why is that?"

You must listen carefully to each response you get because your prospects will often reveal the objection that is going to kill your sale later on. Top 20% reps would rather know this information NOW rather than send out their info, go through the trouble of trying to track them down, go through a long presentation, and then get a no.

Layering questions are effective and powerful and easy to ask. If you want to instantly get better at qualifying, write more of your own and use them.

The Most Powerful Qualifying Question

Your client or prospect has all the answers as to why they will or why they won't buy. As a sales professional, it's your job to uncover that information. You do this by asking the right qualifying questions, by layering those questions, by qualifying any red flags you get and by actually listening to the answers you are given.

While this may sound basic and simple enough, you'd be amazed by how many sales reps still don't do this correctly. There are a ton of reasons why, but in order to simplify the entire process, I'm going to give you the one question that will get your prospect to tell you exactly what they are looking for (and what they're not looking for, as well). And here it is:

During the course of your qualifying, simply ask your prospect:

"_____, if you could wave a magic wand right now and fix (or get) three things that would help your (sales process, bottom line, productivity - whatever is appropriate for your prospect), what would you wish for?"

Now shut up and listen. You will be amazed by what comes out next. My experience is that prospects immediately begin telling me exactly what they are looking for. As I listen carefully, I'm asking myself if my services *can* actually help them, or if they have issues that are outside of my range of services.

If they need something I can't help them with, then I know they are not going to be a buyer. If this is the case, I try to find them a resource and move on.

If, however, they tell me things that I know I can help them with, then after waiting until they are completely finished, I will then give them the good news:

"_____ I'm glad you shared that with me, and I've got some great news for you. The (your product, service, etc.) we're talking about addresses those wishes perfectly, and let me tell you why. First of all...."

I then go over, point by point, exactly how my training matches up with their expressed needs/desires, and I specifically repeat their exact wording back to them as much as possible.

This technique works especially well because it gets your prospect to open up and start talking. And, of course, it gets them to reveal why they will or won't be a deal for your product or service and what you have to do to close the sale.

Five Ways to Keep Your Prospect Talking

The number one skill of a Top 20% producer is his or her ability to listen. Your prospect or client has their own reasons for needing or buying your product or service, but unless you ask questions and shut up and listen, you'll never know what they are. And in today's economy, knowing how to keep your prospect talking is more important than ever.

A Top 20% closer is an expert at asking questions, layering those questions, questioning the red flags, etc., and at the end of a prospecting call or presentation, they can tell you exactly where the prospect stands.

The key here is to keep your prospect talking, and to listen to what they tell you.

Here are five statements you should begin using today to help keep your prospect talking:

1. **"Tell me more."** Simple, isn't it? Yes, but hard to do. Eighty percent of your competition would prefer to pitch, but a Top 20% closer would prefer to listen. Use "tell me more" to encourage your prospects to do just that.

2. **"Go on."** After a prospect appears to be finished speaking, simply say, "Go on," to keep them talking. This works because a prospect likes to talk just as much as you do, but they rarely get the chance when on the phone with a sales rep. Giving them the permission to continue talking is often all they need to do so.

3. **"What happens next?"** This is a great question to use to discover more about the decision process. The good news is that those prospects who answer this will often reveal important information that you can use later on in the sales process.

4. **"What would you ideally like to see happen?"** This is a great way to discover your prospect's buying motives and urgency, if any!

5. **"Oh?"** Phrased the right way, this open-ended word can get your prospect to reveal much more than you might think. Don't be fooled by the simplicity of it. It's harder to use than it looks, and it's more powerful than you'd ever imagine.

Conclusion

You now have a variety of scripts, questions, and techniques that will help you spend more time with qualified prospects. Remember, first we form habits and then they form us. The Top 20% producers find and then use the most effective techniques over and over again, and because of this, they end up spending more time with qualified buyers.

I often say that the sale is usually made during the initial qualifying call, and I think you'd agree with me that if you use the techniques you've just learned above, then you are likely to be generating more qualified leads and calling back more interested buyers. And when you begin doing that, it's much easier to close the sale.

I encourage you to spend some time with the scripts or questions that will work best with your product or service, and then to adapt them to fit your selling style. Print them out, post them in front of you, and then use them. I guarantee that when you do, your confidence will go up, the quality of your leads will go up, you will close more sales, and make more money.

5 | Closing The Sale

How to close more business in less time!

Every sales pro wants to know how to close more business. Unfortunately, most of them won't take the advice I've given in the first part of this book. The reality is, if you want to close more deals, you will have to let go of all of the unqualified prospects in your pipeline.

Once you do, the scripts in this chapter will help you become a Top 20% closer - closing more deals in less time.

The One Thing All Prospects Do

One of the most important things my first sales manager taught me about closing sales is that all the prospects and clients I call back will give some type of sales resistance and will regularly use predictable, worn out brush-offs and put-offs. They'll either use the time tested, "We don't have the time," or "We looked it over and it's not for us," to brush me off. They will also try to avoid making a decision with old stand-bys like, "I'll have to think about it, " or "I'm going to have to talk it over with my boss," or dozens of other objections.

If any of these sound familiar, then the reason they do is because prospects and clients have been using them long before you ever got into sales. And the reason they use them so often is because they work! Even though all sales reps get these same objections over and over again, 80% of closers aren't prepared for them, don't know how to handle them, and are easily blown off as soon as they get them!

I remember my sales manager explaining this to me and asking me, "If your prospects and clients are prepared with scripted brush-offs and objections, doesn't it make sense for you to be prepared with scripted responses to overcome them?" The answer, of course, is yes!

If you want to completely change your experience with closing sales (not only by making it much easier, but also by actually closing more business), then you can do it by simply being prepared in advance for the common objections you already know are coming.

This chapter provides you with the scripts you need to handle most closing situations. Here you'll find scripts on how to deal with and overcome the initial brush-offs you get when you call a prospect back. You'll find scripts on how to immediately ask for the deal and thereby get a good idea of how close or far away your prospect is to making a decision to do business with you; and, of course, you'll get many word-for-word scripts on how to handle objections.

As always, spend a little bit of time with each response and customize it to fit your product, service or selling situation. Once you do, make a commitment to using it on each and every call you make, and I guarantee you that you will be closing more sales starting with your very next call.

How to handle the initial resistance

Let's start at the beginning and address a major frustration for salespeople – calling prospects back only to get blown off by initial sales resistance right at the beginning of the call.

The single biggest mistake 80% of sales reps make when they encounter initial resistance is attempting to overcome it. Let me make this clear right now:

Initial resistance is not to be confused with objections. Objections come at the end of your sales presentation, while initial resistance comes at the very beginning – before you even pitch your product or service.

You have to handle it differently. The key to properly handling initial resistance when calling a prospect back is to simply acknowledge it and bypass it on the way to getting into your presentation. If you don't do this, or if you engage and start trying to overcome this resistance, you'll lose control of the sale and be on the defensive for the balance of the close.

Everyone has sales resistance. Think of your own answer when you enter a store to buy something and are asked by a sales rep if you need help – "I'm just looking" is likely your initial resistance reply. It doesn't really mean you're not interested; it's just your first response. It's the same with your prospects.

So the thing to do is to be prepared for this resistance and have some proven scripts ready so you can easily handle it and get into your presentation. Here are some effective ways to deal with the common initial resistance you run into:

Scripts to Handle Common Initial Sales Resistance

Initial resistance: "I looked it over and I'm/we're not interested."

We're Not Interested - Initial Resistance Script #1:

"I understand, and that's perfectly OK. At first a lot of people I speak with don't fully understand all the ins and outs of this and that's why I'm here. Before you make a final decision, let's do this. I'll take just a few minutes to explain how this might help you, and if, after you understand it, you still think it's not for you, we'll part friends. Do you have that information handy?"

We're Not Interested - Initial Resistance Script #2:

"I didn't expect you to be interested; our marketing department hasn't yet figured out a way to get our potential clients to call us back – that's why they hired me!

But seriously, this (product/service/investment) has some great features that aren't readily available in the (demo/material/information) I sent you and it'll only take a couple of minutes to find out if they would fit and really benefit you.

Tell you what, do yourself a favor and spend a few minutes with me to find out how and if this would be right for you. Grab the information/quote/brochure and let me cover a few things – do you have it handy?"

We're Not Interested - Initial Resistance Script #3:

"I understand and believe me, I get that a lot. In fact some of my best clients said that at the beginning as well. But I'm sure you'd agree that any decision you make, whether it's a yes or a no – and I can take either one – is best made once you understand all the facts, isn't that right?

Well _____, I'm here to help you learn those, so do yourself a favor and grab that information, let's briefly go over it, and if at the end it's not for you we'll part friends. Do you have it handy?"

Initial Resistance: "I don't have the time right now."

I Don't Have Time - Initial Resistance Script #1:

"I know that feeling _____, I've got a lot going on as well. Let's grab our schedules and find some times where we can spend just 10 minutes together. How does later today at, say, 4:30 sound?"

(Keep looking for and make a definite appointment to call back.)

I Don't Have Time - Initial Resistance Script #2:

"That's fine _____, we'll schedule a better time to go over this. Quick question, though: When we do get back together on this, what are some of the areas I should be prepared to go over with you?"

I Don't Have Time - Initial Resistance Script #3:

"That's fine _____, we'll schedule a better time to go over this later. Quick question, though: When we do get back together on this, what are some of the things you like about it? Or, "Where do you see this helping you?"

I Don't Have Time - Initial Resistance Script #4:

"I'll be happy to get back with you when you've got more time. When I do, what areas would you like to know more about?"

Listen and take notes and then make a definite appointment to call back.

Initial Resistance: "It's not for us/me."

It's Not For Me - Initial Resistance Script #1:

"I understand how you feel, and I think you would agree that any decision you make, whether it is a yes or a no, is best made when all the facts are known right? Well _____, I'm calling to help you learn all the facts. You see, I can take a no as well as a yes, but what is important here is that you understand this (program/product/service) completely so that you are in the best possible position to make the right decision--but you get to make the decision! So go grab that brochure and let me help you learn all the facts here. I'll hold while you get it!"

(It is very important at the end here to use an instructional statement. Do not make the mistake that 80% of sales reps make and ask if they will go get the information. You do not want to give them a choice because they will always say no. If they still say no, do not give up! Try other versions of this script.

It's Not For Me - Initial Resistance Script #2:

"It may appear that way now _____, and you may not have enough information or understand it well enough to be interested. In fact, most people I call back feel the same way you do--they think this is (Quickly list one or two perceived negative points), so I don't blame you for not being interested. I wouldn't be either if that were true.

But _____, that isn't how this (product/service) works. To begin with (list two or three benefits that contradict the first couple of negatives you just gave). These are just some of the things you need to be aware of before you make any decision. Do yourself a favor and get that (quote/demo/email/brochure) and I'll show you how this might work for you, too. I'll be happy to hold on while you grab it."

Again, assume that they will go get the brochure, and make sure you end with an instructional statement. If your prospect says that they looked at it, and they introduce another popular objection, like they "Don't have the money right now," remember not to give this, or any objections credence now by trying to deal with them. Rather, answer with another positive reflex response like:

"I understand what you are saying, and most people I speak with don't have money to throw away or put into a bad (investment, product or service). Again though, once I explain how this (your product or service) can actually save you money, (or reduce your overhead, etc.) you'll be glad you invested a few minutes to find out how. Do yourself a favor and grab that brochure – I'll be happy to hold on while you get it."

It's Not For Me (I don't have the money) - Initial Resistance Script #3:

"Let's put the money aside for a minute, because before you make any decision, we first have to determine if this (product, investment or service) is a good fit for you. After I explain a few things about it and answer any questions that come up, then you will be in a much better position to decide if this is something you want to pursue. I'll be happy to hold on while you grab the (brochure or paperwork)."

Remember - the whole point here is that by not buying into their objections by saying things like, "When will you have the money?" Or, "Last time we spoke you said your company could afford this," etc., you will avoid giving all control and momentum over to your prospects.

Initial Resistance: "We looked at your material and this just isn't for us right now."

We Looked Over Your Material - Initial Resistance Script #1:

"I understand, and you know you said something very important. You said right now. I think you'd agree that timing is one of the most important parts of any decision you can make isn't it? Well, right now the timing is perfect for (your investment/product/service).

Before you make any decision, it is important for me to explain how, by acting now, you will (describe a benefit that is important to them). Do me a favor and grab that (brochure or paperwork) and let me explain why. Do you have it handy or should I hold while you get it?"

We Looked Over Your Material - Initial Resistance Script #2:

"No problem, _____. Tell you what let's do – because things change, and while this is fresh in your mind, let's take a few minutes now to match up how this can help you when the timing is better for you. Is that (brochure, quote, demo) handy, or do I need to hold on while you grab it?"

We Looked Over Your Material - Initial Resistance Script #3:

"That's fine, _____. Quick question: When the timing changes, is this a solution that you think will work for you?"

- If No -

"What specifically are you looking for?"

- If Yes -

"Great. What I'd recommend is spending just a few minutes with me now so I can get an exact idea of how to prepare this for you so when you do move forward with it I can have a head start. Do you have that information handy or should I hold while you grab it?"

Initial Resistance: "We already have a supplier or dealer or service person."

We Already Have a Vendor - Initial Resistance Script #1:

"I know and we spoke about that earlier. Remember, I'm not calling to have you replace your current supplier/company. Rather, you were looking at this to see how you might improve the results of what you're currently getting. Tell you what, do me a favor and grab the (demo, information) and let me show you how, if you decide to branch out in the future, this might help you (fill their expressed need from your first call). I'll be happy to hold on while you grab it."

We Already Have a Vendor - Initial Resistance Script #2:

"Yes, I know you do. And that's exactly why I sent this to you. Most companies like yours use several (suppliers, advertising companies, etc.) because each one does a part of the business a little differently and a little better. Since you have our information and we're on the phone now, let's take just a few minutes to see how we may be able to improve (some aspect of their business). If you decide not to move forward at this time, that's fine – at least you'll have some options in case you need to change later on. Do you have that (brochure, e-mail) handy?"

We Already Have a Vendor - Initial Resistance Script #3:

"That's perfect, _____. The best way to see the value in our (service, product, etc.) is to compare the results and ease of use with our product. Do me a favor and grab that (brochure, demo, etc.) and let me show you how easy it is to (save money, improve service, etc.) with a small investment. After that, you can be the judge. Do you have that handy, or do I need to hold on while you grab it?"

We Already Have a Vendor - Initial Resistance Script #4:

"I understand and that's great! You see _____, I only work with companies like yours that are used to using this kind of (product or service). And that is because I know you will really appreciate the (give a benefit here that you know they want) that our (product or service) can offer. Before you make any decision, it is important to see if this can indeed make your job easier. Grab that information and I will cover a few of the highlights with you. Do you have that handy or do I need to hold on while you get it?"

How to Close at the Beginning of the Call

How do the Top 20% close the sale before they even deliver their presentation? If they've done a good job of qualifying up front and the material they sent out explains their product or service well, when they call their prospect back *they just ask for the order.*

Now before you start with your own objections as to why this won't work ("I've got to explain ad nauseam every detail," or "They won't have enough information to make the decision, so I have to…"), just hear me out. First, there are many benefits to just asking for the order right at the beginning:

- A percentage of your prospects will have already decided to move forward with your product or service, and giving them an opportunity to buy or ask some quick questions will not save you a ton of time, but it will prevent you from pitching and talking past the close and introducing new objections.

- Other prospects will be interested in your offer but will have some questions. By getting to these in the beginning, you will save yourself a lot of time and you will immediately be in the closing arena answering buying questions and closing the sale.

- Another group will be hesitant and leaning toward not going with you, and by getting to their objections early, you'll be able to direct your close right at their concerns. This will save you a ton of time and energy pitching things that they have no interest in, and will enable you to tailor your close to their specific concerns – rather than have those come up at the end and kill your sale.

- A smaller percentage will cut you off and end the sales process right then and there. This will save you time chasing, begging, and pitching non-buyers.

Any way you look at it, asking for the sale in the beginning benefits you in many ways and there is virtually nothing to lose. I now use this technique with every sale I go into and find that it has cut my closing time in half, which enables me to move on and find and close more buyers. Plus, it helps me to stay strong as a closer because by asking for the sale right away, I'm able to control the flow and direction of the close. Also, I avoid being ambushed at the end of a long presentation with an obvious negative response that I could have fielded and dealt with in the beginning.

Believe me, this one technique will change the way you currently close sales over the phone.

Three Instant Closing Scripts

Instant Close Script #1:

"Hi _____, this is _____ _____ with (your company). How's your (day of the week) going? Great. Well, I'm sure you received the (quote, demo, information) I sent to you and I'm sure you've gone through it. I've gone ahead and tentatively scheduled the dates (for delivery, or order amounts, or made myself available) that we spoke about last time. What (size order, length of contract, etc.) have you decided to go with on this?"

(Now shut up and listen carefully to which direction you have to go.)

Instant Close Script #2:

"Hi _____, how is your day going? I know that feeling. It's nice to speak with you again. I've been thinking about what we were talking about last week, especially about (state some of their needs you uncovered in the previous call), and I think you'll find that (BRIEFLY give a specific benefit that your product will provide), and I know you'll find that useful.

Now I'm sure you read the information (or spoke with their boss, or whatever they were supposed to do), and my question is – how have you decided to get started with this?"

Instant Close Script #3:

"_____, I've been looking forward to getting together with you on this, and I'm excited to begin working for you. I'm sure you read in the material the part of (your service that is a good fit for them), and I know you'll be especially happy with how that works for you.

We mentioned several ways to begin (state them briefly), and I was wondering which one you decided on?"

Be sure to adapt these scripts to fit your product or service, and always use specific instances of their stated needs when you can. Like all the scripts in this book, get in the habit of using them on each and every call.

One Question to Ask When You Can't Match Price

What do you do when asking for the order from a prospect when he announces that he had done some research and found that a competitor had a lower price for the same service?

He says: *"If you can match the price I'll go with your company."*

The answer is easy when you can match the price, but in most cases you cannot. When this is the case you must uncover the real buying motive. To do this simply ask:

"_____, I'm not saying I can match this price, but if I can, and with all things being equal, why would you go with me and my company and not the other?"

This one question will reveal why he prefers your product, service or company. Once you understand his buying motive, you can leverage it to close the sale right then.

In most cases, the real buying motive will outweigh the difference in price. Understanding your client's real buying motive can often mean the difference between making the sale or not.

Powerful Questions to Keep Your Close On Track

Sometimes during a close, it's necessary to keep your prospect talking. This is especially true when you're not sure how to respond to an objection, or what your prospect or client feels about a specific point or situation. It is times like these that you need to just ask a question and let your prospect tell you which direction you need to go or how you should respond. Use the following questions to help open your prospect up and to get them to reveal where they really stand, and what you need to do to close the sale:

- "I can tell that's important to you; why does it mean so much?"

- "What else do I need to know to understand how this affects your operation?"

- "Let me see if I have this right. You (restate what they said), right? What would have to change for this to work for you then?"

- "Do I have that right?"

- "How would you react if I told you we could handle that and give you this?"

- "Can you give me more detail on that?"

- "What is your perspective on this?"

- "And what has led you to feel that way?"

- "What is your experience with this (solution)?"

- "When was the last time you tried this?"

- "What would have made it work better for you?"

- "If you went ahead with this, what would be the worst thing that could happen?"

- "I hear you saying X, but I'm also hearing something else. Could you elaborate on that please?"

- "And if you didn't move on this solution today, how are you going to change your results and get more (leads, sales, production, etc.)?"

- "Do you see how this (your solution) has been designed to fix your exact problem?"

- "How is this sounding so far?"

- "I see where you're coming from. How did you arrive at that?"
- "What leads you to believe that?"

- "If this did work for you, what would your boss think?"

- "If this did work out for you, what would that mean to you?"

- "If I could sweeten the deal with (give them something extra), would that be enough for you to move on this today?"

- "If you decided to move on this, when is the best time to begin?" Or, "What size package would you begin with?"

- "I'm not sure I understand you. Could you tell me that again?"

- "Go on..."

- "Oh?"

- "Why do you feel that way?"

- "What if that weren't true?"

- "Do you know that to be true for a fact?"

- "Why is that important for this to work?"

- "If this still works given what you just said, wouldn't it still make sense to move forward with this?"

How To Use Tie-Downs To Gain Commitment

One of the challenges you face when selling over the phone is not being able to see the visual cues of your prospects and clients. Working on the phone requires superior listening skills, and you can develop them much quicker if you get in the habit of using tie-downs.

Tie-downs allow you to both gauge and gain commitment from your prospect during the closing process. They also help develop a *yes* momentum. Use the following tie downs during your sales presentation and watch your confidence, control, and closing rate double!

- "Does that make sense?"

- "Do you agree with that?"

- "And that's a nice feature, isn't it?"

- "I'm sure you can see how that would work for you, right?"

- "That's powerful, isn't it?"

- "Do we have an agreement?"

- "You feel that way too, don't you?"

- "Does this help?"

- "Can we get this started for you?"

- "Wouldn't you?"

- "And who wouldn't want that?"

- "Isn't that right?"

- "Are you with me?"

- "You'd have to agree with that, wouldn't you?"

- "Make sense?"

- "Do you see what I mean?"

- "That's what you want to hear, isn't it?"

- "Understand?"

- "You're with me on this, right?"

- "I can't think of a better way, can you?"

- "Right?"

- "Good solution, right?"

- "Agreed?"

- "Sound reasonable?"

- "Got it?"

- "You would, wouldn't you?"

The Real Secret to Closing the Sale

It doesn't matter where I go or what I do, I can't get away from salespeople who quiz me about closing techniques and sales managers who beg me to teach them how to get their salespeople to close.

Everyone in sales is looking for the edge that will help them close more deals. Unfortunately, most people want the easy way out, so they spend their time looking for short cuts and silver bullets which will miraculously deliver huge commission checks. This is why so many questions I get include things like, "What's the trick?" or "Can you tell me the secret of . . .?"

In his oft-cited article "The Magic Closing Pill," author and sales expert Jeb Blount writes:

Universally, there seems to be an unyielding desire to learn the secrets of closing. From superstitions to an endless stream of cheesy techniques, closing, much like putting in golf, is shrouded in mystery. And there is no shortage of "experts" who are quick to claim that they have the one, true secret for "closing the deal every time." There was even a time in my life when I would wear my lucky close-the-deal tie to closing appointments.

Now what I'm about to share with you is a secret that has been guarded by the Knights of the Sales Round Table for thousands of years. It has been passed down from generation to generation – given only to worthy sales professionals who have sworn an oath to use this powerful secret wisely and guard it with their lives. But now, for the first time, I'm going to reveal this secret to the world. But before going further, I need you to solemnly swear to only use this information to earn a higher income, to become sales rep of the year, to go on your president's club trip, to get promoted, and to provide a great lifestyle for your family.

Now get your note pads and pens ready. Here it is. The silver bullet, the real secret, the magic closing pill:

Ask for the business.

Yep, this is the magic pill. **Just ask.** Ask for the appointment, ask for the next step, ask for the decision maker, ask for the business. Ask.

The fact is, if you are having a hard time getting the next appointment, getting to decision makers, or closing the deal, nine out of ten times it is because you are not asking. Why don't you ask? Because nine out of ten times you are afraid to hear "no." "No" stinks and it is in our nature as humans to avoid "no" at all costs. So, we don't ask.

However, because it is fear that keeps us from asking for the business, rather than admitting our fear and working to overcome it, we blame our failure to close on everything else. We blame our product, our company, the economy, our sales manager, our price and our luck.

Instead of owning up to our shortcoming, we look for secrets, tricks, and silver bullets. Instead of facing our fear of "no" and asking anyway, we hide behind justifications like not being too pushy, or bad timing.

Getting past the fear of "no" isn't easy. But the first step is to at least acknowledge that your fear is real. Look, I've been selling for 20 years and have been incredibly successful at it, yet today I still have to remind myself that "no" won't kill me. Once you admit that you fear "no" you can then begin to pay attention to your behavior in front of prospects.

Learn to anticipate the anxiety that comes right before asking for the deal. Then practice overcoming your fear by asking for what you want. When you fail, and you will fail, don't put your head in the sand and pretend it didn't happen. Instead, acknowledge your failure, get back up, and on the very next call *ask for the business.*

Jeb is correct - the real secret to closing is to simply ask for the business. The Top 20% consistently do, while the bottom 80% avoid asking because they are afraid to hear no.

What is important to understand though (and what the Top 20% already know) is that "no," in most cases, comes in the form of an objection.

In the next chapter I'll take you through the process of handling objections and getting to a closed sale.

6 | How To Handle Objections

When you ask for the sale, you will get objections. And while not all products and services are the same, you will find that most objections are. In this chapter you will learn how to identify and isolate your prospect's true objections, and how to respond to those objections and close the sale. I'll provide you with a variety of word-for-word scripts that you can adapt and use to help you overcome the objections you face every day. Included are scripts for objections such as, "I can't afford it now," and "The price is too high," and "It is too risky," and "I want to think about it," and "I'm just going to pass on it," and many more. Sound familiar? They should. You probably get them five to ten times a week.

It's obvious your prospects are prepared with objections that work, so doesn't it make sense for you to be prepared with rebuttals that work also?

Handling Objections in Five Easy Steps

One of the biggest issues for salespeople, when faced with objections, is when and how they answer them. As you've probably experienced, many of the objections you get turn out to just be smokescreens hiding other objections. This is why, when you answer them, you just get another, then another objection. Frustrating, isn't it?

What the Top 20% do to avoid getting this series of objections, is they question and isolate many of the most common objections they get before they attempt to answer them. This is very easy to do and it will instantly enable you to establish control and get your prospect to reveal what is really stopping them from moving forward with you.

Until you know what the real objection is, your closing attempts will be highly frustrating for you, and irritating to your prospects. Using the five-step method will instantly make you a better closer and will allow you to cut through smokescreen objections to eliminate the put-offs and blow-offs that are costing you sales and self-esteem.

Integrate the five-step method into your closing scripts and begin easily handling the objections that are costing you thousands of dollars a year in lost commissions and sales.

How the Five Step Method Works

Step One: Hear them out – completely. The first thing you do when handling objections using the five-step method is to completely hear your prospect out. This is hard for most sales reps because as soon as they get an objection, they fear that the deal is lost, and they think that as soon as the prospect stops talking he will hang up. Because of this, the prospect barely has enough time to get their concern/objection out before 80% of sales reps butt in and starting pitching again.

You must resist this temptation and remain silent while they express their concern. This is a good place to use the mute button on your phone. In fact, if you think there is more behind their stated objection, then un-mute yourself and ask a brief, "Oh?" and "What do you mean by that?"

Doing so will allow you time to think about the best way to handle their objection, and it will often get your prospect to actually give you the answer! You'd be amazed by how many prospects – if you allow them to – will often times either answer their objection, or reveal the real one if you just let them speak. Once again, get very friendly with your mute button and encourage them to say more.

Step One – Part Two: Put in a softening statement. The next part of step one is to address their concern by using a softening statement that lets them know you heard them and that you understand. Once again, you must avoid the mistake 80% of your competition makes, which is to argue or disagree with what they've just said. So often I've heard reps say things like, "That's not how this works," or "This actually offers you a lot more than that..."

Contradicting what your prospect feels is true only puts them on the defensive and makes them want to defend their position even more. Plus, it makes them feel as if they can't really talk to you, and that you're only there to close them and don't care about what they feel is a concern.

The right way to respond whenever you hear an objection or concern, is to always let your prospect know that you heard them and that you understand. You do this by using a softening statement. Always preface any rebuttal with one of the following:

Sample softening statements:

"I understand that."

"I hear exactly what you're saying."

"A lot of my clients have told me that as well, so I understand where you're coming from."

"I completely understand how you feel; this is a big decision right now. I'm sure it makes sense for you to think about this."

"You know a lot of people tell me that as well, so I get what you mean."

Step Two: Isolate the Objection Before Answering It. This one technique of isolating objections is the most powerful closing skill you'll ever learn. Isolating objections before you answer them will eliminate smokescreens and overcome objections, because it gets your prospects to move beyond their initial reflex responses, and often reveal what the real objection is.

In addition, it's the perfect way to handle the most common smokescreen objections you get all the time, like: "The price is too high," and "I've got to talk to (fill in the blank)." Here's how it works with the price objection:

If your prospect says "The price is too high," you simply respond with:

"I understand _____, and let me ask you a question: Assuming the price on (your product or service) weren't an issue (or fit within your budget), is this the solution you feel is right for you today?" Or, "Is this something you would go ahead and move forward with today?"

As you can see, the value of this technique is that it completely isolates the objection and tells you whether it is really what is stopping your prospect from moving forward or if there are other issues as well. Often times price (or whatever reason they give) isn't the only or real objection, which is why when 80% of sales reps try answering or overcoming it, they just get another objection, then another and another.

Use this technique with every objection you can, and you'll be on your way to truly understanding where your prospect is in the buying cycle and how close – or far away – you are from getting the sale.

Step Three: Use a Scripted Rebuttal. Once you've isolated and identified the real objection, you get to deliver a perfect rebuttal to it, because you will be prepared with a variety of carefully crafted and effective scripts. Nothing feels better than being prepared with and delivering a perfect rebuttal. The benefit of using a script is that you get to concentrate on the delivery of the rebuttal – the pacing, the inflection, the emphasis – rather than on what you're going to say.

In addition, the combination of knowing that you're completely prepared with a script that works, and that you're dealing with a real objection, gives you a confidence that separates Top 20% producers from all the others who are fighting with smokescreens and ad-libbing their way through rebuttals that rarely work. In the next section, you'll find a variety of word-for-word rebuttals that you can either use as is, or adapt to fit your product or service. Once you plug them into this five-step method, you'll have a powerful system for handing the objections that frustrate 80% of your competition.

Step Four: Confirm Your Answer. Step four of the five-step method will help you avoid one of the most dangerous pitfalls that most closers fall into, and that is talking past the close. Because 80% of your competition haven't identified the real objection, and because they aren't following a script, what they tend to do is keep talking and pitching past the close. Once they get to the end of their initial rebuttal, they just add on another rebuttal or start explaining another part of their product or service, and this often leads to another big mistake – introducing new objections!

I'm sure this has happened to you as well. In your haste to handle what you think their objection is, you start talking about features or benefits you think they will like, when all the sudden you get a question like, "Is that warranty transferable?" Of course it's not, and suddenly you've given your prospect yet another reason not to move forward with you.

The good news is that by following a script and confirming your answer, you'll not only avoid introducing new objections, but you'll also be getting the green light to then ask for the order again. Use any of the following confirmation statements after you answer any objection.

"Does that make sense to you?"

"Will that work for you?"

"Do you understand that now?"

"Are you with me on that?"

"Do you see how that will work for you?"

Step Five: Ask for the deal. After you confirm your answer, it's time to ask for the order. This might sound obvious, but you'd be amazed by how many times sales people are afraid to ask for the order. There are many reasons for this, including the fear of getting more objections or being told no, but if you are prepared with the five-step method, and you have proven and effective scripts to handle other objections that may come up, then you will earn the right and have the confidence to keep asking for the deal.

The Price is Too High (or) We Don't Have the Budget

Price is the most common objection used by prospects to put off making a decision or get sales reps off the phone. It's also the hardest objection for reps to overcome, because in most instances it's just a smokescreen hiding another, real objection. What usually lies beneath this objection is that your prospect thinks they can get it cheaper somewhere else, or they aren't convinced yet, don't believe in the value, or they don't have the authority (have to talk with someone else) to make this decision.

The problem that 80% of sales reps make is that they believe this is the real objection without questioning it, and so they launch into many unsuccessful attempts to overcome it. This almost never works. Instead, what you must do here is question and isolate this objection to see whether or not it's the real objection, or to find out what is hiding behind it. This is the perfect objection for the five-step method. Here is how easy it is to question and isolate the price objection. Simply say:

"I understand _____, and let me ask you a question. If price weren't an issue on this, would you move on this today and place an order with me?"

How easy is that? Believe me, this one questioning statement will change the way you handle this deal-killer of an objection, and the answer you get here will tell you exactly where your prospect stands. Any answer other than a "yes" means that this is just a smokescreen and not the real objection. If that's the case, then it's up to you to do more probing here to find out exactly what is stopping them from moving forward.

If, however, they say yes, price is the only thing holding them back, then you get to start qualifying on the size of the order, the delivery dates and begin coming up with suitable financing or payment options. Try:

"OK great, _____. Let's work together to get this (your product or solution) working for you today. First of all, where does our price need to be for you to move forward with this today?"

If your prospect gives you a price that you can reach (perhaps a lower one, or one with a payment plan or any other concession you need to make), then before you just agree to terms, you must first get a commitment from your prospect that this is something they are going to move forward with *today* – assuming you can meet those terms. If you can now match the price they are willing to pay, say:

"OK. Now _____, that price (and terms, etc.) are going to need some approval on my end and I'll go get that right now, but before I do, let me make sure that if I can get you (review all the details), then this is something you're prepared to move forward with today, right?"

Only after they agree to the deal should you put them on hold and make the appropriate arrangements. After you've done that, come back on the line and say:

"OK, that's all done on this end, so congratulations. Here's what we need to do now..." Then close the sale.

Twenty Price Objection Responses

Sometimes your prospect might be interested in your product or service, but may not be able to buy all the bells and whistles you're offering, or your price may be beyond what they're willing or able to spend at that time. In this case, you'll need some rebuttals which will get your prospect to open up and talk with you, and give you an idea of what direction you'll need to take to make the sale.

Use these rebuttals, or adjust and adapt them to fit your product or service:

The Price is Too High Response #1:

"_____, one of the most attractive features about this (product or service) is that it actually pays for itself within the first few months because of the cost and labor savings it gives you. After that, it actually makes you money because of the improved production (lead flow, etc.). Let me show you how this works using just one of the examples you gave me earlier. . . (now pitch this again getting their buy-in every step of the way)."

The Price is Too High Response #2:

"_____, money may seem tight right now, but you're focusing on the wrong thing – which is the initial expense. It's true that this will be an investment of ($____) right now, but what you'll gain over the next few months can easily be ($_____). Now I know that if you gave me $1,000 today and I gave you back $3,000, you'd want to do this every month, wouldn't you? Of course you would! So let's do this: Let's start with our introductory (advertising package, starter position, etc.) and we'll base all future investments on the (performance, production) of this one – fair enough?"

The Price is Too High Response #3:

"Let's face it _____, if your car broke down on the way home from work and you had to have it towed and repaired and it cost you the $1,000 we're talking about right now, you'd put it on your card and not even think twice about spending the money. You'd just be happy your car was running again, wouldn't you?

Well the good news is that you can put this (investment, your product or service) on your business card as well and immediately start enjoying the benefits of (extra leads, etc.). You'll pay as little as $40 a month on your card, and as soon as this repays you your investment, you pay the card off and you're still getting the benefit of the improved (lead flow, referrals, your features and benefits). That's how most people begin with this. Do the smart thing and let's get you started right now. Which card are you going to use?"

The Price is Too High Response #4:

" _____, no company or business can grow unless they leverage other people's time, effort and money – you know that to be true. I'm not saying to go into your budget for this, rather, you need to pay for this the way you pay the other expenses of your business – with the bank's money through a business line of credit or business credit card. That's how everyone makes investments to help their business grow.

Now I know you see how this (your product or service) works, right? And I think you'd agree that by using it to (fit their solution), then like our other clients, you too could see the results this generates, right? Then the decision is a no-brainer here, _____. Go ahead and move forward with this and as it (saves them money or makes them more money or leads), then you can do what all the other successful companies do and that is invest even more resources in it as your business grows. Now, I recommend you start with our introductory package of ($____). What is the best card for you to put that on?"

The Price is Too High Response #5:

"_____, people tell me it's too expensive all the time, but I always have to ask, 'Compared to what?' You see, when you compare apples to apples, our (service/product) is far less expensive when you compare it to (X, Y, or Z). When you actually look at the numbers and do the math, we are by far a better value, and offer so much more in terms of return that this is perhaps the most cost-effective solution you'll find for this. And that's what you've been telling me you need – a more effective and cost-efficient solution, right? Then let's get you started with this..."

The Price is Too High Response #6:

"I know our service is higher than other company's quotes, but I'll tell you right now that when I chose to work here, I, too, looked at the competition. And believe me _____, if I thought there was an overall better deal out there than what our company provides you with, I'd be working there, selling that. But there isn't.

You see _____, when you look at what you get with our solution (repeat your unique features and benefits), and you combine the service and attention of our support department, you'll find that we're actually a better value for just a few additional dollars a month. The headaches alone you'll save are worth that. Let's do this...(suggest a starting point and ask for the order again)."

The Price is Too High Response #7:

"_____, I know it ultimately makes sense for you to focus on the long term results of this (advertising plan, etc.), rather than on the initial investment. Once you move forward with this, you'll be thinking about and appreciating the benefits you'll be getting and thinking more about expanding with us. That's why we have so many clients who use and refer us today. Let me quickly go over what just one (part of your solution) can mean to you again, and then you can decide if it's worth it to give this a try, OK?"

The Price is Too High Response #8:

"I understand, _____. Let's just say that I could get you a price that would make sense for you today. Tell me, what other issues would you have to weigh before you would decide to try our trial package today?"

The Price is Too High Response #9:

"_____, even though I know what this (advertising, production, etc.) can do for you in terms of increased business, I know that you're new to it so I wouldn't even let you consider doing what my other clients do month in and month out. First I want to prove what we can do and the good news is that it only takes a small investment to put us to work for you. After we double or even triple your sales results with this, would you agree it would then make sense to consider investing more into this (solution, plan)? Of course it would!

Then let's do this, I'll go ahead and set you up for an introductory account for just $_____. Once this begins giving you (increased sales, a return, etc.), we can talk about a larger position, once again based on the performance you'll see here. Now that makes sense to you, right?"

The Price is Too High Response #10:

"_____, it's always about the money – you and I both know that. But let me ask you a question: what do you think it is worth to you to (increase your sales by 10% a month, save an additional $____, etc.)? If I can show you how to do that for less than half of what it's worth, doesn't it make sense to you to at least try it out for a month?"

The Price is Too High Response #11:

"_____, as a businessman myself, I no longer look at the cost of something. Rather, like you, I know that everything is really an investment. An investment of time, energy, emotion or money. And when you look at it that way, it's never about the money, it's about the return – the results. In other words, if I invest $_____ and this much energy or time, what am I going to get in return? I think you'd agree with that, right?

Well, let's look at this again, and let's stay focused on the results you're going to get. (Now list them one by one.) You see, this is why my other clients use us for this, and I know that it'll make sense for you, too. Let's do this…"

The Price is Too High Response #12:

"_____, whenever you have options, price is usually the first and easiest thing to compare. But the problem is, in comparing price, what usually gets missed is comparing apples to apples. Tell you what I'll do. Go ahead and send me over the other quote you have, and I'll compare it directly to what we're offering you now.

If I find that you are truly getting a better deal, I'll tell you so. If I find that we can match it and even give you a better price and service, then I'll do my best to give you a better overall deal. Either way, you'll win – how does that sound?"

The Price is Too High Response #13:

"_____, I know you have a lot of options out there; heck there are (hundreds of financial planners, etc.) to choose from, so what makes our company and our pricing and services so appealing? The answer is me. Oh, I know, that may sound pompous, but seriously, no one takes their career more seriously than I do, and no one is going to work harder for you than I will.

I'm invested in your success because my family's future is dependent on the results I deliver for you. That's why I chose this company and that's why this is the only solution I feel good enough to invest nine to ten hours a day in. And believe me _____, if it's good enough for me and my family, it's going to work for you, too. Do yourself a favor and put me and my company to work for you today. Like my other clients, you'll immediately notice the difference and be glad you did. Now here's what we need to do..."

The Price is Too High Response #14:

"_____, you know as well as I do, you get what you pay for. I'm sure you can think of several 'bargain' products or services you purchased with a low price that you regretted later on – I know I sure can. That's why when I chose a company to work, for I made sure it was going to give my clients the best value and service, period. I work hard to get new clients, _____, and I don't want to lose them because my product is cheap and doesn't do the job right.

I think you'd agree that when we get you (name the results they are looking for with you), you'll be happy with me and my product and you'll probably be willing to refer us, right? Well, those are the results that sometimes cost a little more, but are way worth it in the end, wouldn't you agree? Then let's do this..."

The Price is Too High Response #15:

"_____, I can definitely lower our price and give you less exposure (or whatever is right for your product or service) and still get you started with us today, but the truth is, that wouldn't be doing right by you. If I can't give you what I know it will take for you to be successful, then unlike other brokers (or agents or companies), I'm actually going to tell you to try another solution. You see, I'm only interested in a win/win situation.

And to make you successful here, our (X package at $___) is the only one you'll be happy with. Sure it runs $800 more, but that additional expense will long be forgotten once you see (improved service, results, etc.). I'd rather do right by you and have a customer for life than short change you just to make a sale today. Can you respect that? Great! Then let's get you started with the beginning package of..."

The Price is Too High Response #16:

"_____, you can always get it (your product or service) for less money. Heck, we could do a Google search right now, and I'll bet we could come up with a few different options that are even cheaper than what you're telling me you can get it for now. The question is – why aren't you going with them? Isn't it because there comes a time when price isn't as important as the loss in quality, service and results?

And that's why our clients keep doing business with us. When you begin getting (the results of your product or service), you'll also understand why our price is worth the value and results you get with us. You can always get it cheaper, but you can't get the results that pay for themselves over and over again. Let's do this...(suggest starting with an introductory package)."

The Price is Too High Response #17:

"_____, when you look around at the competition for this, you'll find that prices are not the same because the quality, results and service you get is not the same. Ultimately, the real decision isn't about price, it's about what you want to accomplish – the results. And _____, I'm happy to say that in that department, we lead the pack of companies out there. Here's the good news – with a small investment of just X, you can put me and my company to work for you and then you can be the judge based on what you get back. Believe me, like my other satisfied clients you'll be back again and again. So let's do this..."

The Price is Too High Response #18:

"_____, many of my first time clients pay for this using the installment options. What you do is simply put this investment in your company on your business credit card and pay the minimum of $40 - $50 per month. And the good news is that with our advertising program (or lead generation, or production saving plan, etc.) you'll see immediate results that could actually pay for your whole investment in just a few months. Imagine being able to finance this, pay it off, and then enjoy the increase in sales and income for the rest of the year! How would that feel?"

The Price is Too High Response #19:

"_____, let me ask you something: Suppose we could find a way to eliminate the cost factor on this; I know right now it's not, but let's just say price wasn't an issue anymore. What other issues can you think of that might stand in the way of you moving forward with this today?"

The Price is Too High Response #20:

"_____, have you ever purchased a cheaper version of something? You know, something that was cheap and plastic, hoping to avoid spending a few dollars more. And do you remember how you regretted it and wished you bought what you knew you should have to begin with? And did you ever have to throw it away and go back and buy the right one?

It's the same thing here. Many of my clients have already tried (our competition or other solutions) and after using us, they tell us they won't make that mistake again. Why not be smart from the very beginning. Let me make a recommendation to you..."

Two - I can't afford it - Objection Scripts

I love it when my prospect tells me they "can't afford it." It leads into these scripts perfectly. Practice these over and over again and deliver them with conviction, and you'll be amazed by your success rate:

I Can't Afford It - Response #1:

"I understand when people say that _____, and I think that what you should realize is that you really can't afford not to participate (or purchase) this now. You see, when you take into account all the money and time you will save by acting now, you could look back on this decision and realize this to be one of the smartest and most cost-effective decisions you've ever made.

A good short term decision to get started now can turn into a great long term decision that will actually make/save you money! So do you and your (company/family) a favor and make the decision to move ahead with this today. What we need to do is.." (Ask for the business.)

I Can't Afford It - Response #2:

"_____, if you think you can't afford to (participate/buy/invest) in this then you actually need it more than most people I speak with! I'm sure you're sick and tired of being broke, and unless you do something about it now, you'll stay broke – and I know you don't want that. Now the bottom line is that if your car broke down on the way home, you'd pull your credit card out and you'd spend (the amount of your product or service) and you wouldn't think twice about it, right?

Well, this is an opportunity to use that same credit card for something that will actually make you money (or give them opportunity or whatever your product or service does), and your investment in this and in yourself right now will save you from being sick and tired and broke six months from now. Isn't that worth it to you?"

Ten - I need to show this or talk to my (partner, boss, etc.) - Objection Scripts

You handle this objection just like you did the price objection – you question and isolate it before you attempt to answer it. This objection, like price, is a classic smokescreen and until you get to what's behind it, you'll get nowhere.

After you hear them out – and this is a great time to use your mute button and pause – put in a softening statement and use the following:

I Need To Show This To Someone Else - Response #1:

"That's perfectly fine, _____. I think you should show this to (whomever they claim they need to show this to). And let me ask you something - if after you show this to _____, and he/she says 'It looks good _____ whatever you want to do,' is this something that YOU would move forward with today?"

Now be aware that any answer other than "yes" means that this objection is just a smokescreen and you haven't uncovered the real objection, and your job now will be to keep qualifying to see what else is standing in the way. Questions like the following will help to bring other objections to light:

"What else might prevent you from moving forward with this?"

- Or -

"What do you think would hold him/her back from moving forward with this?"

- Or -

"What other solutions do you think they are leaning toward?"

On the other hand, if your prospect says he would move forward with this, then you've got to confirm this and make him your ally. Say:

"Great, then I take it you're going to recommend this to _____, right? Wonderful! What can WE do to make sure he agrees with us?"

Do you see how you've now made your prospect an ally and how you are now a team? Listen carefully to what your prospect says, because if they are truly sold on your solution, they might tell you what you now need to do to close the sale. Offer to do a three-way conference call, or to call and speak to the real decision maker directly. Ask about specific follow-up times or additional information that you can provide them with. And always ask what the next step will be and get a definite time frame for following up.

I Need To Show This To Someone Else - Response #2:

"I totally understand. By the way, what is his/her name and position there? OK, and what is their e-mail address? Thanks. Do me a favor and ring their office quickly, I just want to introduce myself – I'll be happy to hold while you put me through."

(If they won't put you through, then make sure and get other contact information about this decision maker – direct dial phone number, extension, etc.)

I Need To Show This To Someone Else - Response #3:

"No problem, I understand. But you are personally behind this, right? So when you speak with (whomever), then you're going to recommend it? Great. Let me ask you this then. When you bring an idea like this to your partner, and let them know you're behind it, what usually happens?"

- If yes, they go with it , then say -

"Wonderful. Here's what I recommend then. Since it takes a few days to arrange delivery/installation/etc., I'll go ahead and get started on putting this order together for you. What size do you think you'll end up going with?"

I Need To Show This To Someone Else - Response #4:

"If the decision were up to you, what concerns or conditions would you change?"

I Need To Show This To Someone Else - Response #5:

"I understand. Let me ask you – how much pull do you have on the final decision? OK, great! And you're going to recommend it, right? Sounds great. When do you think we'll have the go-ahead, then?"

I Need To Show This To Someone Else - Response #6:

"That's fine, _____. Are you comfortable recommending this to him/her? How are you going to recommend (implementing/trying/ purchasing) this? And what will your timeline be?"

I Need To Show This To Someone Else - Response #7:

"_____, let's face it – you're in a position of responsibility because you make good decisions and the (owner/partner) trusts you, right? And you personally think this is a good idea, right? So you've already made the decision to move ahead with this then? OK, I appreciate you need to check with (your boss/partner), but let's at least get the paperwork started so when you convince him/ her that this is something you're behind, we'll be ready to go. Now what size order do you think is best to start with?"

I Need To Show This To Someone Else - Response #8:

"Of course, most of my clients need approval on this before getting started. How can we go ahead and get that approval right now?"

I Need To Show This To Someone Else - Response #9:

"_____, the most effective managers I work with are respect-ed by their bosses because they can think independently and make decisions. That's why they are valuable to their owners. Since you already see the value in this, I think it would go over very well for you to take initiative on this and get the ball rolling. What do you need to do to put us to work for you today?"

I Need To Show This To Someone Else - Response #10:

"That's perfectly OK, and here's what I'll do. I know I gave you the special 10% discount, and I'm willing to honor that price for the next 24 hours until you get approval. All I require from you is a good faith deposit of just $___. That way you can take this to your boss and you'll have some added leverage to get him to see it your way. In fact, he'll appreciate the initiative you've exercised here. How would you like to handle that deposit?"

Ten - I Need to Think About It/Need to Wait Until Next Week/Month/I'll Get Back To You - Objection Scripts

I Need To Think About It - Response #1:

"_____, whenever I tell someone I need to think about it, I usually mean one of three things: 1 – I'm not going to make a deal for whatever reason, and I just want to get them off the phone, 2 – I kind of like the idea but I'm going to have to find the money or talk to my partner, or something else is holding me back, and 3 – I really like the idea and I just have to move something around before I say yes. Be honest with me; which one of those things is it for you right now?"

I Need To Think About It - Response #2:

"_____, I may have given you too much information on the warranty (or pick another part of your product or service here). Is that what you need to think about?"

(Now use your mute button and let them tell you what they are going to really think about.)

I Need To Think About It - Response #3:

"You know _____, if this isn't for you, I'd rather have a "no" right now – believe me, you won't hurt my feelings. Is that where you're leaning right now?"

(It is always better to get this objection out of them early.)

I Need To Think About It - Response #4:

"_____, let's face it – you've already been thinking about this for a long time. You know you have to make a change or nothing else will change with (your operating system, your results, etc.). Thinking about it more won't fix things for you – only making a decision will. You like this; you've already told me it would work for you. So let's do this – go ahead and put me/this solution to work for you now and if you change your mind later you will still get the benefit that you've acknowledged you need. Here's what we need to do to get you started..."

I Need To Think About It - Response #5:

"_____, the only thing more costly than making a bad decision is not making one at all. If you don't change things, then things won't get better for you. Now, you've already admitted that this has the best chance to make a positive impact in your production, right?

Then do what my other clients do and put me and my company to work for you. Once you see the positive results we both know are possible here, you'll be back to expand our coverage for you. And that's going to be a win/win for us both, isn't it? Then here's what we need to do..."

I Need To Think About It - Response #6:

"_____, since we both agree this has a great chance to work for you, let me do this. While we're on the phone right now, I'm going to e-mail you three customer testimonials – companies just like yours who were hesitant at first – and when you read about how successful they were with us, I'll put together an introductory offer that you won't be able to pass up. Once you see for yourself how this works, then we can talk about further involvement -- is that fair?"

I Need To Think About It - Response #7:

"_____, what I'm hearing from you is essentially a "no" – and that's alright. As a sales rep, I hear that all the time and it doesn't bother me. It just means I haven't yet explained the value proposition right. Tell me, what would it take to convince you that this would be a good idea to move forward with – and please be honest with me."

I Need To Think About It - Response #8:

"Perfectly fine. Just to be sure, you do understand how this (your product or service) would work in your environment, right? And are you confident that if you moved forward with it, you would get positive results? And finally, if you decide to give this a try, is the budget there to move forward with it? Then just to clarify my thinking, what factors will you be considering in thinking about this?"

I Need To Think About It - Response #9:

"I understand that, _____. And I know that any business decision needs to be justified in terms of costs and results. I work with businesses like yours all the time and have helped many (managers/owners) in your position analyze the bottom line. And the only place to start is always with what the value of a new customer is worth to your business over the long term. What would you estimate that to be worth to you?

And how many new customers would this have to bring to you in order to justify the investment in it today?

And do you honestly think this would bring you those (two/four – however many they said) customers? Then the answer is easy here…"

I Need To Think About It - Response #10:

"No problem, _____. When should I call you back on this? And what is going to happen between then and now that will convince you to move forward with this?"

Eight - I Already Have a Supplier/We're Taken Care Of/ We're Happy - Objection Scripts

I Already Have a Supplier - Response #1:

"I know you do, and you're the only kind of company we'll work with. You see, my job is providing you with new ways to (save even more, make more, etc.), not introducing new clients into this market. We are a leader in this area, and I am able to offer you the (your type of specific service/product) that you can't get anywhere else.

And for someone like you who already has experience in this market, I know you will be able to appreciate how this (your product or service) will (improve/produce, etc.). Let's do this – we'll start with our introductory account and you can compare the ease of use right alongside whoever you're using now. If you like how we perform, you can consider ordering more next month. Here's what we need to do to get you started."

I Already Have a Supplier - Response #2:

"That's fine _____, and you know I have many brokers myself as well. I have a stockbroker because quite frankly I don't know everything about stocks. I mean, I know the (whatever market you are in) very well, and I know the opportunities and trends that can help make you successful in this (area). But when I want to buy a house, I call my real estate broker. You probably call yours also, don't you?

You see, successful (brokers, companies, account reps) special-ize in their market and so become the best at what they do. You probably do not have a (broker, company, account rep) effectively handling your (investments, accounts, or product) in this specific area, especially not (performing at this rate of return, or saving this much in time and production) as we are talking about here. And that is why diversifying with my company now can do so much good for you.

Let me ask you: If I could (double/improve/lower your costs) by (ap-plying your solution or product), wouldn't you be happy you diver-sified and found a better way of (handling their service/problem)? Then let's do this…"

I Already Have a Supplier - Response #3:

"Yes, I know you do. Let me ask you: When was the last time you sat down and did an apples to apples comparison with your current supplier and the other new solutions/opportunities out there? As you know, technology changes so quickly, and we're able to ac-complish now in a month what other companies take three to four months to get done. Let's do this – we'll do a quick comparison of what you're getting now and what you'll get by using us, and if you have a better solution by staying where you are, then we'll part friends – is that fair enough?"

I Already Have a Supplier - Response #4:

"Isn't it true that the reason you're using your current supplier now is because you believe you're getting the best service and value for the investment and ease of use? And isn't it also true that if their performance dropped off you'd probably begin looking elsewhere to get that solution?

Well _____, when you see how (your product or service) per-forms, you'll immediately feel as if your current supplier's perfor-mance has dropped off – that's how much better we are. Now, I'm not suggesting a total switch, but wouldn't it be prudent to at least see how much more (performance/return) you can get by giving us a try?"

I Already Have a Supplier - Response #5:

"And _____, who were you using before you made the switch to (their current company)? And why did you make that change? And doesn't it still make sense to get the best (return/results/etc.)? Then here's what I recommend we do..."

I Already Have a Supplier - Response #6:

"I know it's a hassle to change suppliers and begin using someone else, but believe me, the little bit of effort you go through in the beginning will save you a lot of time, energy and money over the next few months.. In fact, our clients told us the only regret they had was they didn't make this decision sooner. Here's what I recommend you do..."

I Already Have a Supplier - Response #7:

"_____, why did you choose your current supplier? And now that you've worked with them for a while, what is on your wish list? In other words, if you could make them the perfect solution, what would you change about them?"

I Already Have a Supplier - Response #8:

"_____, there are more than eight supermarkets in my immediate neighborhood, and I regularly go to three of them each week. Why? Because each one does something a little better – I'm sure you know what I mean, right? Well, it's the same way with (your industry). I'm not saying you should stop using your current supplier, rather, I'm just suggesting that you get (your product solution) from the best supplier that you can. That will save you time, money and energy, and I'm sure you're interested in doing that, aren't you?"

Five - Do You Have References/I'm Not Familiar With Your Company - Objection Scripts

Do You Have References - Response #1:

"I'm happy you're bringing that up because it tells me that you understand the value here, that you want to move ahead with it and that you just want to make sure we can do what we've been talking about, right? I mean, if you speak with a few clients who are as happy with our service as I've been telling you they are, then you're prepared to come on board with me, right?"

- Only if YES -

"Great! Then I'll go ahead and do a conference call right now with a few clients and you can ask them all you want and then we can go ahead and set up delivery. Can you hold on for a few seconds?"

Do You Have References - Response #2:

"I'd be happy to let you speak with a few of my clients, but as I'm sure you can appreciate, they are just as busy as you are. If you tried to reach them by yourself, I'm afraid you'd likely play phone tag for weeks. I have direct access to them so I can get right through to them and get you the answers you need. Now, I'll go ahead and conference some of them in right now, but before I take their valuable time, if you like what you hear, what size order are you thinking of placing today?"

Do You Have References - Response #3:

"No problem, _____. I'll be happy to put you in touch with them right now. Let me ask you, when you begin using us as well, if you're happy with our services, could I count on you to be a reference for me too? Terrific! Then let's do this: Let's go ahead and get all the paperwork done on this end; I'll arrange for delivery for you and then we'll take a few minutes to check in with some of our clients. Now, how big of an order are you starting with today?"

Do You Have References - Response #4:

"I know _____, and before I researched and found you, I didn't know you either! That's the good part about business – within a few weeks we can have a relationship that we'll soon wonder how we lived without! Now, I can give you all the references you need, but I think you'd agree that nothing speaks louder than happy and satisfied clients, right? Then here's what we'll do: I'll go ahead and get some on the phone for us now and after you verify what I've just said, we'll go ahead and get delivery planned, sound good?"

Do You Have References - Response #5:

"_____, is that the only thing holding you back from moving forward with me today?"

- If Yes -

"Terrific! Then I'll go ahead and make arrangements to have your order set up – how much were you planning on moving ahead with? Wonderful. Then hold on briefly while I get someone on the phone for you to speak with."

Three - Do You Have a Guarantee/I'm Not Sure This is For Me - Objection Scripts

Do You Have a Guarantee - Response #1:

"_____, I can guarantee you that if I didn't believe this would work for you like it works for all my other clients, then I wouldn't be selling it to you. Getting new clients is hard enough, but if I sold something that didn't work, I'd have to spend my entire career prospecting for new clients – and that is something I will not do.

No, you see _____, I like easy. And because I know this program will work for you, I'm relying on your telling your friends and business associates about it. Let me ask you: If this works for you, would you be willing to give me some referrals?

And that's how I intend to grow my business. But it all starts with results – and that's why I work with (your company), offering our products. Now, what size (order/position/length of contract) did you have in mind today?"

Do You Have a Guarantee - Response #2:

"_____, the only guarantee in life is that if you don't do something different, then things are not going to change. You and I are talking here because you need to (mention the result or the reason they are looking to make a change). And the good news is that we have a solution that is right now working for thousands of other companies just like yours.

I know you're hesitant, heck, that's natural. But until you make a change, I guarantee things won't improve. Let's do this – I'll go ahead and prepare the (size of order and delivery date), and then based on those results, you can decide how much larger of a position you want to take next quarter. Do you have those documents handy?"

Do You Have a Guarantee - Response #3:

"_____, our (product/solution) works for hundreds of other companies who are doing the exact same thing you are now. I guarantee you that if it didn't work, we'd be out of business! I can also guarantee that if you don't begin using us, then you won't get the benefits you know you need. Let's do this, I'll go ahead and prepare our (introductory/starter) program for you so you can get your feet wet, and then based on the results of that, you can decide how much more you'd like to use next month – is that fair?"

Three - We've Already Got More Business Than We Can Handle - Objection Scripts

We've Got More Than We Can Handle - Response #1:

"I know that feeling; we do too! But for some reason, my boss wants to keep it that way, so he thinks it's a good idea to continue to market and introduce others to our products and services. And it's the same way for you as well. Momentum is great, but if you don't keep it going, it will first slow down, then it will stop.

Here's what I recommend: Let's get you started with the (package/solution) as it is, since we both agree it will keep your business coming. And then after the six month trial period, we can reassess. All we need to do to get you started is…"

We've Got More Than We Can Handle - Response #2:

"And _____, I know that the reason you have so much business is because you have the foresight to invest in (your kind of solution). It's actually a pleasure to work with clients like you, because I know you already understand the need for this kind of (product or solution).

And because you already know the value of this, I'm going to recommend you start with us on the professional level that allows you to leverage your way into our top position. That's only (X amount). How do you want to handle payment of that today?"

We've Got More Than We Can Handle - Response #3:

"That's a nice position to be in. And to make sure you stay that way, I'd recommend starting with our mid-level position. That way you'll get X amount of (leads/results) and won't overwhelm yourself. If you find your other (companies offering some similar solution) starting to slip, then you can simply transfer that part of your business into your account here. What I recommend is that you start with (X amount/position) and then increase it over time as you need to. What is the best way for you to handle this start-up account?"

Questioning the Objection

Sometimes I get an objection that I don't have an immediate comeback for. This either means I haven't given my prospect enough time to tell me what direction I need to go to make the sale, or that they're just throwing me another smokescreen. Either way, the best approach here is to simply ask a question and let my prospect tell me what I need to say next.

Doing this will often eliminate a lot of the work you usually go through, and you will be surprised by how many times your prospect will often explain away their objection! It can be as simple as this:

If your prospect says "It costs too much," simply say (and then shut up!):

"It costs too much?"

- Or -

"Compared to what?"

- Or -

"What do you think it should cost?"

- And then -

"What makes you say that?"

- Or if they say "I can't afford it," you simply ask -

"You can't afford it?"

- Or -

"How long will it take you to get into a position to afford it?"

- Or -

"What do you need to do to be able to afford it?"

This process of asking questions is very powerful and will often get your prospect to tell you what is really standing in the way of moving forward with you.

7 | Advanced Scripts and Techniques

I love reading the sports section of the paper because there always seems to be a story on what an athlete or a team does to improve their performance. I read a piece by Peter King from SI.com about his conversation with Ellis Hobbs – former cornerback with the New England Patriots. He was talking about how much respect he had for head coach Bill Belichick.

He said, "Early in my career, Bill called me into his office, and we sat there – for a long time – studying film. He taught me to look for the simple things, and not to make football so complicated. I got better. I was with one of the best coaches of all time, and he helped me become a better player."

In sales, too, you can become a better producer if you concentrate on the simple things and doing them better. Here are two things you can do today to increase your closing ratio and make more money:

1. Keep a record of the reasons your prospects don't close and then concentrate on qualifying these issues up front with future prospects. This was one of the simplest and most effective habits I developed to get better as a closer.

I kept a notebook with all my prospects in it and every time they didn't buy, I'd put, in red ink, the reason why not. I even boiled it down to three codes: NI, for No Interest; NM for No Money; and

NC for Not Controllable. And then I'd keep looking back through my notebook and look for patterns and ask myself, "What do I need to focus on and change during the qualification stage?"

If too many prospects were not buying because they simply weren't ready to buy right then, then I knew that "No Interest" needed to be addressed on the front call a lot harder. I'd start by asking more questions like:

"_____, if you find that this would work for you, what is your time frame for moving ahead with it?"

And so on. Bottom line – if you don't get it right on the front end, then you'll never increase your closing ratio. Again, concentrate on the simple things, and as you do, your results will improve.

2. Ask for bigger orders on every close. I know you've heard this before, but how often do you actually do it? Many salespeople are afraid to ask for more and are just happy to get a minimum order. I know because I used to be that way!

My career turned around when I began asking for big orders on every single call. What I learned is you never know how much a person or company will buy until you ask. (You can always go down in price, quantity, etc., but you can rarely go up.)

The truth is, it's the same amount of work anyway, so why not ask for two times, or three times the minimum order and see what you get? If only one in ten of your prospects buy the increased amount, how much more money would that mean to you?

The fun part about consistently asking for more is that you'll end up getting more – and every time you do, your confidence improves. As you get a taste for closing bigger deals, you begin looking for and expecting them. Try it and you'll see for yourself – it's one of the simplest things you can do to make a lot more money.

So there you have it – two simple ways of closing more business and making more money. Just remember, as you're reading this, top athletes and coaches are working on the simple things to improve. You should be doing so, too!

How to Stay Firm on Price Using the Takeaway

I've already given you a ton of scripted responses on how to handle the price objection. Now I want to address what to do when you have no negotiation room to lower your prices.

In today's economy, everyone wants a lower price. I'm getting e-mails and calls every week from salespeople around the country who want to know what they can do to deal with prospects and clients who are looking for discounts and even threatening to take their business elsewhere.

"I can't go any lower," they tell me, "and certain clients just keep low-balling me and working me for more discounts. What should I do?"

If you are dealing with this sort of thing as well, then I've got some specific advice that will not only work for you, but will make you more confident and successful as well. To start with, you have to admit the truth:

> *You can only go so low with your price, and some people will buy, and some won't - period. Continuing to lower your price not only cuts into your commissions (and company margins), it also doesn't always work, as you know. And the worst part is that after you've jumped through all the hoops and your client still doesn't buy, you feel used and abused.*

That feeling is even worse than not getting the deal, because it kills your confidence and makes you a weaker closer. After a few days or weeks of taking that weak attitude into your calls, your prospects begin to hear that defeat in your voice and you will keep getting beaten up over and over again.

Want a better way? Adopt the attitude of the Top 20% and do what they do. To start with, the Top 20% know that the two greatest feelings in sales are:

- Getting a deal, and
- Keeping control of the close by using a takeaway and leaving the call with strength.

The Top 20% know that not all prospects and clients are going to buy, and they know that staying strong and using a takeaway is the only way they can leave the call successfully. Here is what they say after they have made their best offer and the prospect/client is still trying to get them to go lower:

"_____, I totally respect that you're trying to do what's best for your company right now, but the offer I've just made is the best I can do and still give you the (level of service, quality, value, etc.) that you'd expect and be happy with. If you can get this somewhere else and it fits within what you're willing to pay, then I'll just have to understand and hope that I can work with you next time. I'm here for you now, but the decision is up to you – what would you like to do?"

Many times, calling their bluff like this will get your prospect or client to stop hammering you for price and sign up. And those who walk? They would have walked anyway, and now when they do, you will have remained strong. Just like the Top 20% do.

How to Build Value

You hear it all the time -- if your price is higher than your competition, you're told to "build value." You're instructed to stress the quality, the warranty, the features, etc. But your prospects have heard all that before, haven't they? Want a better way?

Let's face it, prospects will often buy from people they like, know or trust. Your enthusiasm for your product or service is also a big factor in getting your prospects to place an order with you as well. Knowing this, I've often used the following script to not only build value in my product or service, but also to build value in myself. Here's what to say:

If your prospect says, "I can get it cheaper," or "Well, the XYZ company has something similar or for less money," or anything like that, say:

"You know _____, I'm aware of all the other options for this (product or service) and quite frankly if I thought any of them were better for my clients, I'd be working there and selling them.

When I got into this industry I did my own research, and I looked for the best company that not only offered the top (product or service) but also delivered exceptional customer service and follow-up. I chose (your company) because they give my clients the best over-all value and the best experience, and that means they continue to do business with me and refer new business to me as well. Believe me, if there was a better product or company for you to be doing business with, I'd be there and we'd be talking about that. But there isn't.

Bottom line -- if you want the best overall value, results and experi-ence with this (your product or service) then do what I did – choose (your company). You'll always be glad you did. Now, do you want to start with the X size order or would the Y size order be better?"

This technique builds value in the most important part of any sales transaction -- you and your belief in your product or service.

How to Find Out What's Stopping Your Prospect from Buying

Do you have any prospects in your pipeline that seem to be dodging you? Or should I say, how many prospects do you have like that? I get e-mails all the time asking me how to get a pros-pect/customer to reveal what's really going on. Many sales reps write that after multiple calls, messages, etc., when they do get the prospect on the phone, all they get are vague answers. If this has ever happened to you, then here's how to deal with it:

The first thing you need to do is realize that if your prospect isn't calling you back, or if when you do reach them all you get are vague answers or more put-offs, then you probably already have your answer. They aren't a deal. It's time to move on!

The problem with 80% of sales reps is that they will chase and chase unqualified prospects because it seems easier than cold calling and looking for real buyers. "At least they took the information, or have a need," they say.

Perhaps, but are they buying? Usually not. And all that energy and time you waste chasing them makes you a weaker closer.

The solution is to ask the tough questions! In other words, when you do get them on the phone, ask them point-blank where they stand and if you're still in the running. Try this:

"_____, let me ask you a question and please be honest. We've talked about this now for X amount of time (or -- You've had this information for X amount of time), and I don't want to keep bothering you if this isn't a fit for you. But I do need to know if this looks like a solution you actually think you're going to act on, or if you have something else in mind? "

Now shut up and listen. Because you have given them an out, they will usually tell you the truth. Your job now is to listen to it and learn from it. Just because they aren't buying doesn't mean you can't get stronger as a closer.

You see, whatever reason they give you for not buying -- budget, not a right fit, staying with their current supplier, their accountant won't let them do it – whatever the reason is, you need to take this as a lesson and begin qualifying for this more thoroughly on all of your subsequent prospecting calls (see the previous tip on two simple ways to improve).

This is one of the most important habits you can develop to improve as a closer. This is how the Top 20% get stronger and better - by learning and improving on each and every call. Remember:

1. If a prospect or customer is avoiding you or is being vague, then you probably already have your answer. They aren't doing it. Be prepared to move on, but first:

2. Ask the tough questions and give them an out (use the script

above).

3. Listen and learn from the reasons they aren't buying from you and work this into your qualifying script for all subsequent cold calls. Remember, you can only close prospects who are truly qualified, and it is your job to qualify them.

Meeting Objections Head On

As I've said before, most of the time objections are just smoke-screens hiding the real reason your prospect isn't moving forward. You know this to be true. Many times, when your prospect puts off making a decision, they will give you some objection that you can't overcome, and when you try to deal with that one, you just get another and another.

We discussed how to question and isolate objections previously, but sometimes you've got to just take an objection head on. In other words – call your prospect's bluff. Here's how this works with the most common objection: "I'll have to think about it." When you get this (or another similar) objection, say:

"You know _____, whenever I say that to a sales rep I really mean that I either don't fully understand it, or I'm interested but not sold on it yet, or I'm really not going to move forward with it.. Which is it for you?"

This is a great way to handle this objection, because it gives them a way out. They will either tell you they really are interested and what they need to think about, or they will level with you and keep you from wasting any more valuable time. Either way, you win.

I recommend you use this kind of approach whenever you get an objection you feel is a stall or serious smokescreen. Meet it head-on! Wouldn't it feel better to know the truth now than to spend weeks chasing and begging?

How To Build a Foundation of Commitment

Prospects go through many phases before making the final buying decision. Some sales have more phases than others, and there can be many steps involved, including evaluating data or demos, going up or down the decision chain, talking with partners, spouses, or others, etc. Whether your process is short or long, your challenge is the same – how do you get buy-in and commitment at every phase of the process, thereby building a foundation of commitment that leads to an effortless close?

The answer is by asking direct, specific questions that require your prospect to either commit to what's next, or reveal that they are not qualified. (I know you hate to hear that, but it's better to find out sooner rather than later). Here's how you do it:

First ask a commitment question at the end of your qualifying call before doing anything else. If you know you're dealing directly with the decision maker, then use the question below and adapt it to fit your specific selling situation:

"_____, I'll go ahead and (get this demo/quote/info off to you) and let me ask you a question. If you can see how this will/can (state the benefits and match them to their specific needs), is this something you will take advantage of (next week or whatever time frame you've discussed)?"

Now, if there are many other layers involved, then you need to get a specific commitment on what will happen next. So you should say:

"Terrific. I'll go ahead and get this off to you so you can begin your evaluation process. Let me ask you again: Based on what we went over (restate their specific needs and exactly how your product/service fits these), does it sound/look like this might be the solution your company is looking for?"

- And then -

"What can you see that might get in the way of us moving forward with this?"

You may be thinking that you don't want to introduce an objection here. Don't worry, you are not. What you are doing is exposing possible *red flags* that will only get worse as you go through the sales process. It's better to know *now* what potential problems might come up.

During any phase of the process, it's crucial that you continue to ask specific, direct questions. Here are a few that will always help you know where you stand – and what you need to do next:

For example, if they say, "Well, the XYZ department has to look at it now," you say:

"Great. Does that mean that the 'other team' has approved it?"

- Or -

"That's wonderful. How much closer to a decision are we?"

- Or -

"Who do I need to speak with in that group?"

- Or -

"And what happens after that?"

- And -

"If they agree (like it), are we a go?"

- And -

"What could go wrong there?"

- And -

"How many other proposals are they looking at?"

- And -

"Where does ours stand," Or, "Who are they leaning toward so far?"

- And -

"Are *you* still onboard with this?"

As you can see, what all these questions have in common is they require a definite answer. This is something the Top 20% demand to know and that the other 80% are afraid to find out. The questions above put you in control of the sale.

Trial Closing Questions To Use During Presentations

These questions will vary from taking a prospect's pulse to see if they are with you, to finding out if a benefit you just listed would work for them, all the way to a trial close. They will give you the feedback you'll need to close the sale.

1.   After giving any part of your presentation, you can ask, "Are you with me so far?" You should vary this with, "How does that sound?" Or, "Do you see what I mean?" and, "Does that make sense?"

Always listen carefully to not only what they say, but to *how* they say it. And always allow a few seconds after they respond to give them time to add something else.

2.   Any time you give a benefit, ask, "How would you use that?" or, "Could you use that?"   Or, "Would that work for you?"   Or, "Would that be of benefit in your situation?"

Again, LISTEN to what and how they respond...

3.   Throughout your presentation ask, "Do you have any questions so far?"   This is one of the best questions to ask, and it's also one of the least used.   You'd be amazed by the kinds of questions you'll get, and each one reveals what your prospect is thinking.

4.   Trial closes are always good – "Does this seem to be the kind of solution you are looking for?" or, "How is this sounding so far?" or, with a smile in your voice, "Am I getting close to having a new client yet?"

Even though that sounds cheesy, you'd be amazed by how it will often break the ice and get your prospect to lower his/her guard.

5.   When you finish your presentation, always ask, "What haven't I covered yet that is important to you?"

This is a great way to end your presentation, because if they tell you they don't have any questions, then you get to ask for the order.   If they do have questions, you answer them and then ask for the order.

The bottom line is that asking questions -- and then shutting up and listening -- is still the most effective technique in sales.

How To Close On Call Backs

One of the biggest mistakes salespeople make is failing to close on call-backs. The sad thing is, call-backs are often the best time to close. It all starts with what you say when you call a prospect back to close the sale.

First, here's how 80% of sales reps begin their closing calls:

"Oh hi, this is _____ with the XYZ Company. I'm calling to follow up on the (proposal, information, etc.). Did you have a chance to review that?"

Another equally weak opening most sales reps use is:

"Hi, this is _____ with the XYZ Company, how are you? Good, I was just calling to see if you received the demo we sent to you?"

This is the worst way to begin a call-back! First, you're giving all control over to your prospect. Second, you are opening yourself up for a stall or put off: *"No, I haven't had time yet. Why don't you call me back next week?"*

If you want to be a Top 20% closer, strike the phrases "Just calling to follow up" and "Just wanted to see if you..." out of your pitch – FOREVER!

Here is how the Top 20% open their call-backs:

"Hi _____, this is _____ _____ with the ABC Company. You know, I've been looking forward to getting back with you and getting you started with our (award-winning newsletter, number one industry ranked product, world-class service -- fill in your product/ service/investment here). I know you'll be as happy and satisfied as my other clients are.

Now, I'm sure you've (read the brochure/watched the demo, etc.), and I'm sure you see how it can help you (give a benefit they are looking for). My question is, do you want to start with our starter position of _____, or does the professional _____ position work better for you?"

Now shut up and listen. This script works because:

- First, you're asking for the deal right away (and you'll be surprised by how many are ready to buy on the spot!)

- Second, it immediately starts the close on an assumptive and positive note.

- Third, you eliminate introducing any put-offs and stalls.

- Best of all, you immediately get the prospect to tell you where they stand and what they're thinking, and what direction you need to go in order to make the sale.

While this technique may seem simple, don't underestimate its power. Don't be afraid to use it with each prospect you call back – you will never scare away a real buyer! What you will do is expose all those non-buyers who now take up your time and drain your energy. Wouldn't you like to know who they are up front?

I guarantee that if you begin using this approach on every sales call, you will be well on your way to doubling (or more!) your closing percentage and income.

How to Save a Sale

Recently I was speaking with a new prospect who had called in to inquire about one of my inside sales training programs. I went over her needs, matched up my training to fit those needs, gave her the price options and began closing on dates.

That's when I got the old stall, "Well, let me run this by my boss, and I still have to hear back from blah, blah, blah." Sound familiar?

What was worse was that a few days later she stopped returning my calls and didn't respond to my e-mails. Now, I can take a hint, and I know that she probably wasn't going to be a deal. I'm sure you can relate, so I want to give you a proven technique that will allow you to:

- Open up the dialogue again.
- Find out why your prospect isn't going with you.
- Get them to tell you what you can do to save the sale (if possible).

It's called the "I love to learn" technique and here's what you do:

First, you are going to have to be persistent and keep calling your prospect until you catch them and they pick up. *Don't leave any more voicemails.* Once you get them on the phone, say the following:

"Hi _____, I'm glad I reached you – how have you been?"

- They will likely try to brush you off here, so you say:

"That's perfectly OK. I've been in sales long enough to know when we might not be a fit for a company. Just a quick question, though. You know, I love to learn and I'm always trying to improve. Could I ask you what specifically about our (offer, quote, product or service) didn't seem right for you?"

Now shut up and listen! If you do this right, your prospect will tell you what was wrong with your proposal, and this will give you a chance to adjust or adapt it to fit their needs. Will it always work? Of course not, but if there is still a chance to get a deal, this technique will show you how.

If it doesn't get this particular deal, it still does something very important for you – it gives you the information you may have missed when qualifying this prospect. That means that you can be even more thorough in this area with the next prospect. Make sure to take specific notes here and turn these into questions to add to your qualifying checklist, and watch your closing percentage go up as a result of getting out more qualified leads.

Straight Selling – The Quickest Path to the Top 20%

What's one of the biggest differences between the Top 20% and the bottom 80%? The bottom 80% are still using stale, phony techniques that don't work, and they are still trying to trick the gatekeepers and assistants as they try to get to the decision maker.

All this does is identify them as another pesky sales rep trying to sell something the prospect doesn't want.

The Top 20%, on the other hand, have found that by being honest and real – I call it "Straight Selling"- they not only differentiate themselves from their so-called competition, but they are also able to make a real connection and to establish the kind of rapport that is crucial for any sales transaction. Here are a couple of scripts you can use to begin practicing straight selling:

If, while cold calling, your prospect says they are not interested, use this response:

"I don't blame you_____, you've never heard of me and you don't know what my company does or how it can help you. I'm sure you get sales calls all the time, but I'm also sure that sometimes a call turns out to be truly worthwhile. This happens to be one of those calls..." (Now provide a benefit, or ask a question.)

If you reach an assistant and are told they will take a message, say:

"You know _____, I'm sure you work closely with _____, right? Great. Listen, I'll be honest with you – I don't want to bother you by calling and calling trying to reach _____, so let me tell you why I'm calling and you can tell me if you think this would be something he'd be interested in hearing more about…" (Now ask qualifying questions to see if they'd be a fit.)

If your prospect is avoiding you after you've sent info, or is putting you off, when you finally reach them try:

"_____, I'm glad I finally reached you, and let me ask you something and please be honest with me – I've tried to connect with you several times, and the timing just never seems to be right. Level with me – is this just something you're really not interested in at this time, or do you sincerely want me to schedule another time later to go through this with you. You tell me." (Now shut up and listen to their response.)

As you can see, these straight selling techniques will not only give you the respect you deserve, but they will separate the buyers from the non-buyers. And that is one of the most important top 20% techniques of all.

The "Instant Close" Technique

When I was on vacation in Hawaii, I met a salesperson for Starwood properties. She was selling ownership units (used to be known as timeshares) for one of the more beautiful properties on Maui, on Kaanapali Beach.

She told me a little about the great value of the properties, about what a wonderful company she worked for, and then she explained how all the prospects went through a presentation, before she, as a salesperson, got to work with them (close the sale).

I asked her if she would be interested in learning one powerful technique that could increase her closing percentage and eliminate much of the work she was doing. She was all ears.

I told her that if I was selling this ownership opportunity, the moment I sat with a couple after their presentation I would ask just one question:

"So, are you ready to make one of the smartest decisions of your lives and become an owner of one of these amazing properties, or do you need me to help you make this decision?"

I'd then shut up and listen. This "instant close" technique works because:

- It's a trial close.
- It tells you exactly where the prospect stands.
- It reveals how much work you will have to do to get the sale – or not!
- It gets right to their main objections.
- It saves you an enormous amount of time and energy, and it guarantees you won't talk past the close or introduce new objections.

The best part of this technique, though, is that you can use it on virtually any sale, with any product or service, and it works.

The Most Important Word in Sales

A real estate agent told me an interesting story about their office's top producer. He was talking to her one day and asking her what she did that made her so successful. She said her secret could be summed up with one word.

NEXT!

I agree. The majority of people you speak with, I told him, are never going to be a deal. The problem 80% of sales reps make is they spend time with them anyway, sending information, making multiple appointments, and begging and chasing the deal. In many cases they are afraid to let go.

The Top 20%? Their attitude is - NEXT. I'm here to tell you it's this attitude that separates 80% of sales reps from the Top 20%! The Top 20% know when to say NEXT, and they aren't afraid to say it.

Prospects are either qualified or they aren't. If they're not, then it's best to end the call on your terms and go into the next call with some power and confidence. You'll only do that if you're willing to say NEXT.

Asking For Referrals

I know you've heard about the importance of asking for referrals, but I bet you can't remember the last time you did. Asking for referrals from both clients AND prospects is an advanced Top 20% technique. I say advanced because many top producers forget to do it consistently, but those who make it a habit are rewarded month after month with new business. Here's how to do it properly:

The important thing to remember is to be assumptive. Not, "Do you know of anyone..." Instead say:

"_____, first I want to thank you for your business. I know you have options out there and I appreciate your trust in me and my company. Like your business, mine grows by word-of-mouth, and so I'd like to ask you – who do you know who would also appreciate the (benefits of your product)?"

Now shut up and listen.

Top 20% producers also ask prospects for referrals. That's

right, even those who don't buy! Try:

"I understand _____, and thanks for being so nice with me. I'll follow up with you in a few months. In the meantime, many people I speak with often know of others who might need or want (your product or service). Who do you know of that might be a good fit for this?"

The point here isn't that everyone will give you a referral, but that you ask for one! The most important thing about asking for referrals is to make a habit of it. Practice asking each person you speak with for a referral.

How To Deal With Prospects Who Say - "I Can Get a Better Deal Elsewhere"

Today's business world is competitive. Besides the normal objections you get (no money, price too high, need to talk to _____, etc.), a common objection that blows out 80% of your competition is, "I can get a better deal elsewhere." This frustrates a lot of sales reps and takes thousands of dollars of commission out of their pockets.

The Top 20% also get this objection, but are prepared for it and know how to overcome it. Here's what they do:

First, they recognize that if someone says that they can get a better deal elsewhere, it means one of three things:

1. They're wrong (in other words, they think they are getting the same thing you are offering, but they're not);
2. They're just putting you off and using this objection as a smoke-screen;
3. They really can get a better deal.

In order to find out what your prospect means, offer to help them determine if they really are getting a better deal by questioning and comparing every component of it. Use this script:

" _____, my customers tell me this all the time, and sometimes they genuinely can get a better deal, but a lot of times they can't. I'll tell you what I'll do. I'll go over each item you've been quoted by this other company, in other words I will compare apples to apples, and if everything is equal, I'll see if I can do even better on that. If I can, you'll get an even better deal and if I can't, I'll tell you so. Either way, you'll win. Now, do you have that other quote in front of you? Great. Go ahead and (fax/email) that to me and I'll go to work for you on it."

Then simply go over each item to make sure everything is equal. Often times it's not and you can point this out. And if it is, you still have a chance to win the deal. If they do have a better deal, then build the value of having you as their sales rep and try to close the sale anyway. Either way, you'll win.

How to Get the Re-order

I've listened to thousands of recordings sent to me over the years and what is glaringly evident is how unprepared most salespeople are to ask for more business when calling back existing customers. Here's how the majority of them open their call:

"Hi _____, this is _____ with the ABC company, and you order X supplies from us. Just wondering if there was anything you needed..."

Or,

"Just wanted to see how you were doing with your supply of..."

These calls rarely result in a re-order. The key, when calling back existing customers is to script out and plan your call in advance. You want to assume the sale and lead your customer to a re-order. Try these scripts:

"Hi, this is _____ with the ABC company. We of course supply you with your X equipment. I was looking at your account and I see that it's time for you to order (your new model or replacement)."

- Or -

"And I see you must be getting ready to order some more X equipment,"

- Or -

"And I see you must be running low on X product."

- And then immediately suggest an order:

"I see you ordered X amount with us last time, would you like us to ship you that same amount, or do you need more than that today?"

**- Regardless of what they say, be ready to suggest
another product or promotion:**

"You know I'm glad I reached you. We're having a special today on Y, and they seem to be flying out the door. Would you like me to send a box of these out to you as well?"

Remember, be assumptive and suggest an order. The more you do, the more orders you'll get.

The Most Powerful Close in Sales

The most powerful close, in sales and in life in general, is the *take-away*. The reason it works is because:

We all want what we can't have.

You experience this all the time. Have you ever been to a restaurant and tried to decide between several items? As soon as the waitress tells you the X choice is sold out, what do you want?

Try it with your kids. Give them three options, two of which you know they want and one that is only so/so, then take that one away. Guess which one they will cry over?

It's the same in sales. I was once coaching a client, and he was telling me about an objection he kept getting and I gave him the rebuttal for it. "What happens if they still object?" He asked. Take it away, was my response.

By taking it away, you will either build interest or you will call your prospect's bluff and get a non-buyer off the phone. Either way, you will do something even more important -- you will leave the call in control and with confidence -- and that's the second greatest feeling next to getting a deal. It's a Top 20% feeling.

Here are some examples of the takeaway. Adapt and rewrite them to fit your product or service:

"_____, this product/service isn't for everybody. The companies/people who do use/buy/order/invest in it already understand the benefits and wouldn't use anything else. If you don't understand them now, you probably will later. If there are any available then, I'll be happy to offer them to you but they are selling out quickly at this price. It doesn't matter to me if you buy later at the increased price, or if you get it now at a discount – it's up to you..."

- Or -

"_____, if you're looking for someone to tell you not to do this, then I'll tell you now – Don't do this. Feel better? OK, now that the pressure is off both of us, let's talk seriously about what you're missing out on..."

- Or -

"_____, it doesn't matter to me if you take this now, because I've got ten other clients waiting for my call. They already understand the value here and will close this out whether you do it or not. It's for your benefit, not mine, that I'm offering this. You tell me, do you want to make a great decision now, or should I just give someone else a call – you tell me?"

- Or -

"_____, there are only X cases of this left, and it doesn't matter to me if you buy them now or if the next client buys them. Somebody will in the next hour or so. If you'd like to wait, that's your decision. Should I just call _____ and offer it to them?"

- Or -

"_____, either you get the value of this or you don't – I'm not here to twist your arm. I'd be happy to call you back in six months, and if we have this product/price/special available then as wel,l you can act on it. I doubt we will, but it is up to you. Do you want to move ahead with this now or should I just offer this to (your competitor)?"

The important thing is not to worry if they don't buy – some people won't! Just don't beg a deal, ever. Instead, use these and other takeaways and stay strong -- you'll be glad you did.

The Most Important Script You Will Ever Use

I get many requests each month for phone scripts. People want to know how to open the call, how to avoid being blown off, how to handle objections, etc. While I've covered all this in this book of phone scripts, there is one script that every sales rep needs to use every day.

Now get ready because it actually doesn't have anything to do with the objections listed so far. Nope. Rather, it is the script of what you say to yourself over and over throughout the day.

Here's the Real Top 20% Secret -- top producers are top producers because that's how they see themselves performing. They have a picture of themselves -- a self-image -- as a top producer, and it is this picture that determines their actions and their results. They have a "winner consciousness" and it is this attitude that will always determine their results. Period.

You should know this truth right now -- you're not losing sales because the market is bad or because the product is overpriced or any other external event for the situation. If you're not succeeding, it's not because your territory isn't very big or good, or because the leads suck. Nope. It's all about your self-image and what you expect of yourself. What you believe is what will become true for you, always.

This is proven over and over. As Dr. Robert Anthony says in his book, *The Advanced Formula for Total Success*:

"Your ability to accept is determined by your consciousness. We all know people who have more money than they know what to do with, and we all know many people who never have enough. Why the difference? If a person who has virtually nothing is given a large sum of money, within a very short time that person will have nothing again. If we divided all the money in the world equally, in a short time the rich would be rich again, and the poor would be poor.

Many people think that if they could just get their hands on a large sum of money, they would be set for the rest of their lives. This is absolutely not true. Surveys have shown that people who receive large sums of money without working for them -- those who won lotteries, or inherited wealth, for example -- almost always find themselves back to their original financial level within two years of their windfall. They think that if they had money, they would pay their bills, get out of debt and start anew. But that very seldom happens. Over ninety percent of the people who win large sums of money eventually end up with no more money than they had before their winnings. Their standard of life does not increase and it is, in many cases, lowered because of their excess spending. The point here is that if you have a poverty consciousness or a consciousness of lack and limitation, you will literally spend yourself into poverty. If you find yourself with too much money, you will spend whatever you have in order to get back to your comfort zone.

Take all the money away from a person who is a millionaire -- one who has the consciousness of a millionaire today -- and within a short time he or she will be a millionaire again. Riches start from the mind, not your pocketbook, bank account or investment. The bank account and investments are the effects, not the cause. The cause is always an idea or belief. A person is not rich because they have money. They have money because they are rich in consciousness. They believe that they are rich. Again, this is the reason that the rich will always get richer and the poor will always stay poor until they change their consciousness."

This is powerful stuff because we all know it is true. I have experienced this personally, because I used to have a poverty consciousness and my results were that of a bottom 80% producer.

But that all that changed when I used the following script or affirmation to change my subconscious picture and self-image. I recommend you copy and rewrite or adjust it to fit your product or service, and then write it down on a 3" by 5" card and then affirm and visualize it with emotion and feeling three times a day.

I guarantee that if you do this, your results will change. It will be the most important script you'll ever use:

$55,000 GROSS PROFIT PRODUCTION (whatever sales production you want)

"I feel so powerful now that I am closing more business. It's like me to qualify each prospect thoroughly, and I often uncover their exact buying motives. I'm a powerful closer and if my client says no, that's when I go to work -- I listen for my opening and I use all the right scripts, rebuttals, and closing techniques. And it's working! I'm closing more sales, making more money, and I love seeing my name on the deal board over and over. I knew I could do it and this feels great."

I used the above affirmation consistently, with emotion, and within 90 days I was the closer of the month out of 25 reps in the office. And I have never looked back. And you can do it, too. The bottom line is that you're always going to be affirming and building your subconscious picture of yourself. Is it going to be a poor or rich picture? It's always up to you.

Use the above affirmation or create your own, then visualize it, feel it and watch your sales take off. It works, it really does.

Conclusion

You now have a variety of techniques, word-for-word scripts and strategies that you can begin using to immediately improve your success selling over the phone. Any one of these scripts can and will make you a stronger, more confident closer, and the more you use them, the better you will become. If you make a commitment to learn, practice and incorporate these scripts into your sales calls, you will be surprised by how easy selling actually is.

Scripts are meant to make your job a lot easier, not harder! Remember the analogy of your favorite actor or actress. They study their lines, become intimately familiar with them and then they concentrate on the delivery, timing and pacing of their material. It should be the same way for you as well. Concentrating on the delivery of your scripts and presentation will allow you to form a true connection with your prospects and clients.

In addition, using scripts will allow you to do something even more important. It will allow you to truly listen. Once you know exactly what you're going to say in all the sales situations you find yourself in, you'll be prepared to listen to not only what your prospects are saying, *but to what's behind what they are saying.* And once you learn to do that, you will be in the top 1% of all selling professionals in the world.

BONUS SECTION

Industry Specific Scripts

No where does the 80/20 rule apply more than in Real Estate. In fact, I'll bet you can name the top producers in your office, can't you? The question is, what do the Top 20% do that enables them to achieve consistent results? More importantly, what can you begin doing today to move into that elite group of top producers?

This bonus section is designed to give you the most effective and up to date responses to the most common objections you get when speaking with real estate prospects. In fact, these responses are the word-for-word answers that many Top 20% producers are using right now to close more sales and earn more money. Here are scripts for the top ten objections in Real Estate:

Objection #1: "I'm going to try to sell it myself."

"Some people do try and do that at first, and in a seller's market, that works about 25% of the time. In a market like today though, well, I guess it's theoretically possible, but the odds are really stacked against you. I'm assuming you're going to advertise it in the paper and then do some open houses?

- If yes -

You know _____, I don't want to discourage you, but what you're describing is passive marketing. Unfortunately it's what a lot of people in your position do, and they end up losing a lot of time and money and hiring an agent in the end anyway.

_____, smart sellers put me to work for them in the beginning because I do what's known as active selling. That means making 50 or more phone calls a day to lists of buyers and contacts in my database and using the contacts of other agents in my office.

It's why my closing rate on homes is over (80%) even in today's market. When you think about it, isn't that the kind of success you're looking for, too?"

- If yes – schedule an appointment -

- If no -

"I understand, and I want you to do what's comfortable for you. Let me ask you a question: If you need to reach out to an agent down the road for any reason, could I be the first one you call? Great, then grab a pen and write my number down where you'll have it handy.

-Try for control here to see if they are real – then give them your information. Then ask:

I'll also follow up with my other contact information. Where should I send that?"

Objection #2: "My best friend (brother, uncle, etc.) is an agent."

"_____, we all have friends (or family members) who are in the business, and there are plusses and minuses in doing business with friends and family members, as I'm sure you're well aware. My experience is that it's usually best to work in business with someone I'm not related to. It's the best way to keep a good relationship and get the best business results. And any business decision should be based on bottom line results.

Now _____, like all my clients, I know your most important goals are getting the best price for your home, and actually finding qualified buyers who can purchase it in a timely manner, right?
What I'm going to suggest is that I meet with you to explain why my close rate on homes is (85%), while the average of other reps is just 40% or less. Are you available to meet at four o'clock today, or could I make an appointment with you for tomorrow?"

- If you still get the "I'm going to use my friend" then -

"I understand, and I want you to do what's comfortable for you. Let me ask you one last question: If you need to reach out to another agent for any reason, could I be the first one you call? Great, then grab a pen and write my number down where you'll have it handy.

- Try for control here to see if they are real – then give them your information. Then ask -

I'll also follow up with my other contact information. Where should I send that?"

Objection #3: "We're not ready to buy at this time, we're just looking."

"I can understand that, and I know you'll keep looking until you find something that's just right for you, won't you? Well that's what my job is – to help you look until you find the right house or situation for you. Have you ever done any house shopping before?"

- If yes -

"Then you know it can take quite a while to find just what you are looking for – which is why it's important to always be on the lookout. Let me ask you a question: If I kept my eyes open for you and actually found just what you were looking for, when would you be in a position to move on it?"

- If not for a long time or "I don't know," then do some probing and ask questions like -

"Are you committed to moving into this area down the road?"

"What is your realistic time frame for that?"

"Would you like me to contact you when I find something that meets what you're looking for?"

"OK, one last question: When you are ready to seriously start looking, could I be the first agent you call? Great, then grab a pen and write my number down where you'll have it handy."

- Try for control here to see if they are real, then give them your information. Then -

"I'll also follow up with my other contact information. Where should I send that?"

Objection #4: "What's your commission? That's too high! So-and-so will do it for less." (Variation: "I don't want to pay full commission.")

(Note: This objection usually follows a weak presentation or perceived weakness on the part of the agent. Many buyers will attempt to test you with this objection. Your job? Remain strong and use the script below.)

"_____, the only agents who cut their fees are the desperate ones who also cut the price of your home at the negotiation table. I don't do either. I work 12 hours a day for you and my assistants work 10 hours or more to find the right buyers and negotiate the best deal for you. I don't compromise on my service, and I don't sell your house short. That's the kind of agent you want representing you, isn't it?"

- If no -

"OK, I will respect your decision on that. If your house doesn't sell, or if you're not happy with the results, can I be the first agent you call? Great, then grab a pen and write my number down where you'll have it handy."

- Try for control here to see if they are real – then give them your information. Then -

"I'll also follow up with my other contact information. Where should I send that?"

Objection #5: "I can't afford to sell." (Variation: The values aren't strong enough for me to sell now.)

Note: If this is a true statement for your prospect, then they are not a qualified prospect. Use the "Could I be the next one you call" script. But first question the objection using the questions below.

"I understand. Let me ask you, under what condition would you sell your home today?"

- Or -

"What would motivate you to sell your home in this market?"

- Or -

"Under what circumstances would you consider selling today?"

- Then, leave with -

"Fair enough. I want you to do what's comfortable for you. Let me ask you one last question: When you are ready to make a move, could I be the first agent you call? Great, then grab a pen and write my number down where you'll have it handy."

- Try for control here to see if they are real, then give them your information. Then -

"I'll also follow up with my other contact information. Where should I send that?"

Objection #6: "I have to find a home to move into before I will decide to sell."

"Of course you do, and that's why it's so important to start the entire process now. You see, selling your home and finding and buying your new one are part of a joint process – you do them both at the same time.

That's because while it may take a couple of months to find the right buyer for your house, and perhaps 60 days to complete the paper-work and make the transfers, what you don't want to have happen is to find a new home and not already be in the process of selling your existing one.

The last thing you want is to have your new home sold from under you because you haven't attracted a buyer for your old one. This is one of the most common mistakes people make – and I'm sure you can see why...

What we need to do is sign the listing agreement today, so we can begin the work of finding your new home, while simultaneously find-ing the appropriate buyer for this one. In addition, while I'm looking for your new home, I can also begin promoting your existing one to all the new buyers I'll be in contact with. By the way, if I find a few homes for you this weekend, would you be ready to go have a look at them?"

- If yes -

"Terrific! Then let's take care of that listing agreement, and I'll go to work for you today..."

Objection #7: "Well, the other agent is willing to list for _____%, so I want you to do so as well!"

"_____, if I asked you to list your house for $25,000 less to make it easier for me to sell, you wouldn't like that, would you? You'd start wondering what was wrong with me, and you'd start to question how good of an agent I was, wouldn't you?

Well, that's exactly what you need to begin asking yourself about any other agent who is willing to cut corners to get your listing. You see, these are usually the kinds of agents who are not very good at what they do. They're usually struggling and they're looking for the easy way to make a sale, and that's bad for you when they start negotiating with someone like me.

You see, I'm not only going to sell your house, but I'll protect you as well and get you the best deal all the way around. And isn't that what you're really looking for? Fine, then let's go ahead and take care of this listing agreement and put me to work for you today…"

Objection #8: "My home is worth way more than that!"

"I totally understand what you mean by that, and if people bought homes based on what they should go for – meaning the intrinsic value and the work and time you put into it – then we'd have a completely different market out there. But we don't.

The real estate market works on comparables and comparative values. I'll get you the best value for your home in this area, I can assure you that. And I can get you the best value on your new home when you're ready to move.

The bottom line is no one can do better for you today than me, and my track record speaks for itself. My recommendation is to put me to work for you, and to do that you just need to make a decision and sign the listing agreement..."

Objection #9: "Selling is a big step and we need to give this more thought. But if you have potential buyers, bring them by." (Variation: they want the agent to present a 'verbal offer.')

"_____, I agree, selling your home **is** a big step and you should think about it. The last thing you want to do is waste your time entertaining low-ball offers, or leading people on waiting for an offer that's never going to come.

Believe me, if you knew the kind of time and effort that's required to bring qualified buyers to your home, you'd understand why nobody is going to do that for you until you're absolutely ready. Now, when you do decide you're ready to move forward, then I've got a marketing strategy and a marketing team that will be ready to move into action for you. Realistically, when do you think that would be?"

- If, "I don't know, or, if I see an offer I like then I'd move on it" then -

"_____, I don't work part time. Some agents might, and with them you'll get a part time result. It'll be a long, drawn-out process with ridiculous offers that will just frustrate both of you. I'm sure your time is more valuable than that. Let me ask you up front: If I had a qualified buyer who would pay a good market price for your home, would you sell today?"

- If yes -

"Great. Because that's my job. Here's what we need to do to get that qualified buyer to you...." (Get them to sign the listing agreement!)

Objection #10: "We aren't in a hurry."

Note: You must question this objection to find the way in. Try:

"What would have to change for you to consider entering the market and selling your home today?"

Now, based on what they say, you'll have ways to open up the close. An alternative to this can be:

"_____, when I tell people I'm not in a hurry, it usually means I don't have a buyer who is ready to pay what I'd like to get for my property. Let me ask you this: If I had a qualified buyer who wanted to buy your property for a fair price, would you sell today?"

If No, then you've got a non-qualified prospect on your hands – walk away using the "Could I be the first agent you call" script.

- If Yes, then -

"Great! That's my job as the top agent in this area. By putting me to work for you today, I will immediately go out and begin finding those buyers for you. What we need to do first is get a listing agreement signed…" (Close the sale.)

Bonus Section #2	How to Overcome the Top Ten Objections in Financial Services

I began my career selling investments over the phone, and I know how hard it is to compete with someone a prospect may already be doing business with, as well as how hard it is to get someone to trust me – especially if the transaction is made over the phone. When you add to this the volatility of the marketplace, the availability of securities on sites like Schwab and E-Trade, it can be tough going!

The good news is people still like to do business with people, and when it comes to the dizzying array of financial products, they still need advice and the special support and direction only you can provide them. Here are scripts for the top ten objections in financial services:

Objection #1: "I already have a broker"

"Of course you do _____, that's why we're speaking today. I only work with experienced investors like you – my job is introducing my clients to new ways of (making money, saving on taxes, etc.), not introducing novices to the marketplace.

And as an experienced investor, I'm sure you know how important diversification is, right? Well, _____, diversification includes your financial advisors as well. I know this may sound a little silly, but it's analogous to how doctors specialize. I mean, if you have kidney problems, you go to a urologist; and if you need surgery, you don't go to your general MD, you go to a surgeon right?

Well it's the same thing with financial advisors as well. You see, we specialize in (your type of investment), and that's all we do (that's the majority of what we do/that's the area I specialize in). Your current broker may have your mutual funds covered, but if you want expert advice on how to (save money on taxes, make money in the foreign market, etc.) then that's where I come in. Now let me ask you..."

Objection #2: "I'm just not moving on anything right now"

"I can appreciate that _____, and you know you just said something very important -- you said "right now." I think you'd agree that timing can sometimes be one of the most important parts of any investment you'll make, right?

Well _____, the timing for this (your type of security or plan) couldn't be better. You see because of the (list the reasons why the timing is perfect right now) we're recommending that you put at least (a percentage) of your portfolio into this now. The good news is that even with that amount you can still take advantage of the (benefits again).

Plus, you'll get to begin a relationship with me and my firm, and that, in my opinion, is the best part of all my client's portfolios! (smile in your voice) So here's what I recommend we do..."

Objection #3: "I don't know you" or "I don't feel comfortable doing business over the phone"

"_____, if doing business over the phone is hard for you, I completely understand – it's hard for me as well. I wish I could meet all of my clients in person, and many of them I do. But what I've found is that the best relationship builder is good, steady performance. And that's what all of my clients – both in person and over the phone – get from me.

_____, let me ask you something: If we begin a relationship today and I help you get the kind of results we're talking about here – isn't it true that you'd be happy, whether we meet by phone or in person?"

- If yes -

"Then let's take the first step and put some of your portfolio to work with me and my firm today. You'll always be glad you did. Now did you want to start with the X size position, or were you more comfortable with the Y size?"

Objection #4: "Sitting on the fence"

If your prospect is "sitting on the fence" and you just don't know where to go, it is important to instill confidence and trust. You should use a close here that stresses building a relationship. Try this:

"_____, you seem a little hesitant right now, and I can understand how you feel. Taking the first step in anything new is often difficult. But it's important for you to realize that I am on your side in this. We are in this together. My goal is to put you into a (program/ product/vehicle) like this that will (earn/provide you) with the results you are looking for. And it only makes sense that if I can perform for you like I do for my other clients, then you, too, will want to (reinvest or reorder) with me and my company for many years won't you?

And that is my main concern. Now _____, I'm not saying that you should start with a large order that will be uncomfortable for you. Rather, just start with enough to put my company and me to work for you. We can then base all other participation on the successful results we achieve here. That makes sense, doesn't it?

Great. Would you like to start with X order, or would Y order be better for you?"

Objection #5: "I'm going to wait for the market to recover/get better/stabilize/etc."

"_____, more money has been lost by people trying to time the market than by any other reason. The fact is, smart investors make money regardless of what the market is doing and that's because they invest in companies with solid fundamentals and they back that with prudent research and an overall game plan. And that's exactly what I do for my clients.

Now there are many ways to approach today's market – dollar averaging, leveraging, straddles, etc. And based on what we've gone over for you, I'd recommend you (present your recommendation). Let's approach this in a way that will make you comfortable, but let's not miss out on putting your money to work for you now. Would you like to start with X amount, or would Y be better?"

Objection #6: "Multiple choice close"

One mistake 80% of your competition makes is asking for the minimum order and being happy and satisfied when they get it! Because you never know how much a prospect or company can handle, you should stop robbing yourself of thousands of potential dollars by selling yourself short. By using the multiple choice close, you can avoid this. It's easy to use and goes like this:

"_____, some of our clients start with the minimum (investment/ position/order) of $100,000 and usually wish they had taken more, while others realize that with a (vehicle/investment/offer) this good it makes sense to move other things around to get the budget and so participate at the $250,000 to $500,000 level. And of course our professional investors wouldn't even consider anything less than $1,000,000. Where do you see yourself starting off?"

Now sit back and let them tell you how much they can and want to do!

Objection #7: "Setting the appointment"

If you spend much of your day calling and trying to set an appointment, then try using one of the following scripts to quickly establish interest. Just remember, your job here isn't to try to create an interested and qualified lead. Rather, your goal is to find those prospects who might be interested in meeting with you. That's why you'll find these scripts to be short, to the point, and pretty direct. Your goal is to get feedback from your prospect as soon as possible.

"Hi, is this _____? Hi _____, this is (your name) and I'm a financial planner with (your company). How's your (day of the week – or morning/afternoon) going? Briefly, I'm calling to introduce myself and let you know of a (vehicle/plan/product) that is (saving/earning/sheltering) my clients (%), and I was calling to see if you'd be interested in meeting with me to see if this could help you as well..."

Now, pause here and gauge their reaction. If resistant, see some of the resistance scripts in a previous section.

- Or -

"Hi, is this _____? Hi _____, this is (your name) and I'm a wealth management specialist with (your company). How's your (day of the week – or morning/afternoon) going? _____, we haven't met yet and the reason I'm calling is simply to introduce myself and to see if you'd be open to some of the ways (your current offering/special products) can help you (save on taxes, earn income). I'd be happy to spend a few minutes in person with you next week to see if this would fit in with what you're trying to accomplish. Would you be open to that?"

Objection #8: "It's too risky"

"_____, it's obvious that we're not talking about a CD that will give you a three percent return or a real estate fund that might give you six percent if everything is going well in the economy. Now I'm not saying that those are bad vehicles – they have a place in every portfolio, of course.

But you know as well as I do they will not give you the growth, the protection against inflation, cost of living, etc., that every portfolio should have. For that you need the (investment/vehicle) we're talking about here.

Now I'm not saying you should put all of your money into this. What I am saying is to be smart. Diversify a portion of your portfolio into this (your specific vehicle or investment strategy), and put yourself in the position to keep the kind of lifestyle you're used to. The last thing you want to do is worry about the future – especially at this stage of your life, right? Then here's what I recommend we do..."

Objection #9: "Your fees are too high"

"You know _____, if you just look at our (two percent management fee) and ignore the value, the return, the guidance and the peace of mind you get for that fee, then I imagine it doesn't seem worth it. But when you look at the overall value, the lack of ongoing trading fees, and the growth of your portfolio that we can offer, then you come to appreciate what our other clients do – you're getting a great service, backed by a network of professionals whose sole job it is to protect and make you money.

When you view it like that, it becomes a real bargain. And when you factor in the time you'll save, the worry you'll give up, and the ease of living you'll have knowing your portfolio and future is being professionally safeguarded and protected, then you'll be happy to pay that fee, and refer others to me as well.

Let's go ahead and do this – put a portion of your portfolio to work with us today, say just $500,000, and let me show you how much we can do for you. Let's go ahead and..."

Objection #10: "I've lost money with you guys before"

"Gee I'm sorry to hear that. Tell me about it... Well _____, we all lose some money when we invest, but the key is to have a sound overall strategy so we can always make more than we lose. Now I'm not perfect, and a small portion of your account may have some down months along the way – that's only natural.

But I'll tell you this: after we put together a plan that fits your risk tolerance and your personal goals, I'll make sure that you're in the best position to not only achieve the return goals we set, but also in securities that are sound fundamentally so you can avoid the losses you've had in the past.

Can I guarantee you'll make a lot of money? No, and nobody can do that. Can I guarantee I'll work as hard with your money as if it were my own? You can take that to the bank – along with the returns I'll help you realize. So let's do this..."

Bonus Section #3	# Power Closing Techniques for Mortgage Brokers

Much of the time in mortgage sales, the struggle is to get your prospect to agree that it makes sense for them to listen to how you can help them. There can be many reasons prospects don't want to go through changing their current lender, and there are just as many reasons why it makes sense for them to do so. Your job is to open the door to a conversation and to get them to open up long enough for you to explain why it is in their best interest to listen and do business with you. Use the following "Power Closing Statements" to open and close the sale:

Power Statement #1:

"_____, most people I speak with don't realize how many options they actually have when it comes to today's loans. Let me ask you – if I could get you qualified and approved for the best loan possible, and have it done by the end of this week, would you at least make a commitment to take a serious look at what I can put together for you?"

Power Statement #2:

"_____, people tell me all the time that they can go to their bank for this, and that's true. But let me ask you something: If I could save you literally thousands of dollars on your loan by shopping it to dozens of lenders who are motivated to earn your business, wouldn't you be interested in at least seeing what I could do for you?"

Power Statement #3:

"Are you familiar with the unique system I use to find you the best loan in today's market? I (Briefly explain your process or the details of your unique product). And let me ask you this: If I can save you thousands of dollars, and make this a fast and enjoyable process, would you at least allow me to show you what I can do for you?"

Power Statement #4:

"_____, I'm not saying I can save you money or get you the best deal on your loan yet – I'd have to do some work on it first. But I can say this: I'm committed to helping all my clients get the very best offer and deal out there, and I have the resources and experience to do that. Now let me ask you something: I'm willing to commit to finding you the best offer out there. Will you give me your commitment now that if it fits your needs, saves you money and is easy to do, you'll then put me to work for you?"

Power Statement #5:

"Now _____, I know you have a lot of options out there, but I can guarantee you that you can't get what I can offer you anywhere else. First of all, I'm committed to finding the absolute best deal out there for you, and I have relationships with all the best underwriters available to you today. Second, I have several unique ways of getting your loan to fit your needs and still save you thousands of dollars. And third, I can usually get an answer by the end of the week so this process can be quick and painless.

My only question is how serious are you in moving forward if I can find the exact loan that works for you?"

Power Statement #6:

"_____, most people don't put very much thought into a major loan like this – they just go to their bank because it's convenient and they end up giving thousands of extra dollars to their bank that they could have kept in their pockets. Every one of them would have done better if they had just done what you can do right now – simply take a few minutes to let me explain how I can save you a pile of cash and smile each and every time you write that loan payment every month. Now let me ask you this..."

Power Statement #7:

"_____, don't you owe it to yourself and your family to find out how to keep literally thousands of dollars in your pocket? I mean, if I can show you in just five minutes how to save a ton of money from going to your bank, wouldn't it be worth the time to find out how?"

Power Statement #8:

"_____, you wouldn't want to work with someone who would lower their commission, because they are the same agents who don't have the strength to fight for you and get you the best loan.

You see, I work for you and defend your loan terms when I negotiate with the lenders out there, and they know that I'm not going to back down and lower my standards. My job is to get you the best loan that will save you thousands of dollars, and that's why my clients do business with me.

You do want a strong broker negotiating and working in your best interest, don't you?"

Power Statement #9:

"_____, I'm not here to waste your time and if I can't get you the best loan out there and save you a pile of money doing it, then I'll be the first to tell you to go elsewhere. And all I ask of you is that if, after we spend a few minutes together, you don't like something about what we come up with, you tell me now so I can make adjustments or move on. Is that fair?

So after we come up with an agreement today, I'm prepared to commit to working for you and getting you these terms. My question is: Are you prepared to commit to putting me to work for you today?"

Power Statement #10:

"I can definitely save you a ton of cash on this loan – I do it all the time. And I'm willing to put my time into this for you, research for you the best deal, negotiate for you the best terms and deliver to you the absolute best deal you can find anywhere. My question to you is simple: If I can get you the loan that makes sense for you, is there any reason you might have for not moving forward with it?"

Bonus Section #4

How to Overcome the Top Ten Objections in Insurance

The good news about insurance sales – like all other sales – is that the set of objections and put-offs you face is essentially the same. In other words, day after day, in presenting your products and services, your prospects probably come up the same old objections they've been using for years. Things like, "I'm happy with what I've got," and "I'm healthy and that won't happen to me." Because of this, you have a distinct advantage if, and this is a big if, you have taken the time to prepare in advance for these objections and then have practiced your responses so they sound easy, natural and convincing.

Below you'll find ten rebuttals to these and other common objections you get when closing on your insurance products. Remember, take the time to reword or rework them to fit your specific services or selling style.

Besides the confidence you'll get from being prepared for these objections, having these prepared responses will allow you to relax behind what your prospect says and actually listen to what they are trying to tell you. Again, your prospect will always tell you what you need to do to get the sale – or why they will never buy – and unless you're truly listening, you'll never hear it.

Objection #1: "I'm happy with who I have."

"I'm glad to hear that _____, and I'm not here to come between the relationship you have with your current broker. Instead, I'm only interested in making sure you have access to the best new vehicles to fit where you are in your life now. You see, the issue with most insurance is that people tend to buy it and forget about it. And the problem with that is that life, situations and responsibilities change and in most cases the insurance coverage gets neglected.

Let me ask you this: When was the last time you had someone look at your existing coverage and compare it to what's now available based on where you are in your life today? Well here's what I'm prepared to do for you – I'll compare your current coverage and your current needs with what's available today, and if you have the best coverage at the best rates, then I'll tell you so. And if I have a better vehicle at a better rate, and it makes sense to you, then you can decide what to do. Either way you'll win. Is that fair enough?"

Objection #2: "It won't happen to me"

"_____, when was the last time you totaled your car? (usually never). But you still have it insured for that loss, don't you? You see, that's the thing about insurance – we buy it to protect us in advance in case something happens that we couldn't afford to cover. If we never use it, we're grateful, and if we have to use it, we're thankful. Either way, insurance gives us both protection and peace of mind.

Now _____, if (the situation that you're insuring for now) did happen, how happy are you going to be that you have coverage for it? (probe here – "How would that affect your wife? What would that give her in terms of time with the kids, etc?")

_____, the little bit of premium you pay now provides you and your family (or business) with a great deal of comfort and security.

It's the right thing to do and I think you know it. Let me ask you this: What kind of (monthly/quarterly) payments are you trying to stay within – perhaps I can adjust your policy or length of term to make this work for you..."

Objection #3: "Why change what I have?"

"I'm not saying you should change, and it may not make sense for you to change – that's why I need to do some work for you to see if I can help you. You see _____, most brokers write an insurance policy for their clients and then they're off to make the next sale. What they don't do is what is perhaps the most important part of all – continue to assess their client's changing needs and match them up with a newer vehicle that would get them more appropriate coverage – perhaps for even less money.

And that's what I'm here to do for you today. Let's do this: I'll take a look at what you've currently got in terms of coverage and premium, and I'll compare it to what your needs are today. I'll then review what is available to you, and if there's a better fit for you, I'll let you know about it. If not, then I'll let you know that as well. In the end, you get to decide what's best for you. Is that fair?"

Objection #4: "The price is too high"

"_____, let's put the price aside for a moment and talk about the coverage and what you're trying to accomplish. Can we agree that based on (review their needs) you think this is the right (insurance vehicle, policy, product) for you?"

- If no - Then you've got other issues and will have to keep qualifying -

- If yes -

"OK, then we have a couple of options here and they are to either reduce the length of time (term) or the coverage amount in some area. Which do you feel more comfortable with? And what premium range are you trying to stay within?"

- Rework the policy to fit within that and say -

"OK, you can still get (give details of the new policy) and that will only run you $____. What I recommend you do is start with it this way and if or when things change for you down the road, we can revisit this and perhaps increase your policy. In the meantime, what's important is that you get coverage now. Here's what we need to do to put this policy into effect today."

Objection #5: "You all think you can save me money."

"That's a good point _____, but for me it's not all about the money. You see, my real concern is that you get the right amount of coverage first, and then get the best rate possible on that as you can. You see, I tell my clients that if they were on a cruise and the ship sank, what's important isn't the size of the life boat, but whether it had holes in it – you with me?

Now _____, I may or may not be able to save you money, and I'll let you know that soon. What I can do, however, is offer you the best coverage with the least headaches. After I match up what you're trying to accomplish with what I find to be the best vehicle for you, then we'll talk about whether I can save you money or not. And if I can, great! If I can't, I'll let you know that, too.

But first, let's get you a nice, safe, stable and dependable life raft that isn't going to sink just when you need it. After we do, you can decide if you want to purchase it or not. Is that fair enough?"

Objection #6: "Life insurance sales."

"_____, life insurance is one of the most important and yet neglected insurance vehicles there is. Heck, nobody expects to die prematurely, yet we all know of people who pass every day before their time. I suppose you do as well, don't you?

Well, while it's a sad thing when we hear about that, what we often don't tend to think about is the family that is left behind in the following weeks and months. I mean, where would your family get the money to handle the bills, pay the next six months' mortgage, the ongoing weekly expenses? Would they have to move? Who would watch the children and who would pay for that? And don't forget that all these decisions would have to be made while dealing with the overwhelming sadness of missing you…

_____, while providing your wife (spouse) and children with a place to live, food on the table and some security while they figure out how to go on with their lives won't ever replace the loss of your presence, but it will make that transition easier and provide the space for them to begin putting their new lives together. Believe me, they will ALWAYS be grateful for the decision you're about to make today."

Objection #7: "No hurry"

"You know _____, we're never in a hurry to buy insurance until something happens. It's an interesting product that way. In fact, it's the only product we buy and hope we never have to use! I'll never forget a story one of my clients told me (either come up with your own real example, or use this one that actually happened to me!) of when he decided to let his motorcycle insurance lapse because he was selling it. It was a great, big, expensive bike, and he put ads in the papers and took calls on it.

Well, sure enough, one morning he woke up and went out back and all that was left of his motorcycle was the chain that used to secure it to a pole in the ground! He told me of how he called his insurance company and told them he forgot to send in his policy check and then borrowed a car and drove fast to make that payment before the grace period ended.

You see _____, you're never going to be in a hurry to buy insurance until something happens – and then it's always too late. Right now we've got this policy that is perfect for you, you can afford it and you (and your family/business) need it. Do yourself a favor and put it in effect right now while you can and it makes sense to. Tomorrow morning could easily be too late. Here's what we need to do..."

Objection #8: "Have insurance at work"

"That's great _____, and many of my current clients do as well. The reason they still take out a policy with me, though, is that there are many limitations to the insurance you have access to at work, namely the fact that it's only good while you're working there. And in today's job climate, it only makes sense to have stand-alone coverage.

Also, the rates at work are usually averaged over everyone and you get lumped in with the rest of the employees. That usually means you get less coverage than you're paying for.

Tell you what we should do. Without obligation to you, would you be interested in at least knowing what your options are in terms of getting quality coverage that is designed to fit your and your family's needs? I mean, I'll give you all scenarios including price, length of term and coverage. After that, you can compare it to what you have access to at work and then make your own decision – is that fair?"

Objection #9: "No budget"

"_____, I can certainly understand that and here's what I suggest: Let's look at what you're currently paying for this (if they are – or "Let's look at your need for this), and I'll do some research on my end and come up with something that you can afford at this time. It may or may not be all the coverage you need, but what's important is to get something in place that you can add to when things change. Is that fair enough?"

Objection #10: "Why now?"

"_____, someone once said that the best time to buy insurance is when you don't need it. In fact, it's only good when you do need it and that's always when it's too late! Let me ask you, how's your (health, business, car – whatever type of insurance they need) right now?

- If OK -

Great, then this is the day you want to make the decision to get covered. And the good news is that since you're (OK, things are going well, etc.) I can offer you the very best rates and coverage on this. Now, given what we went over, you said that a (describe the type of coverage and details) would work for you, right? Then what I recommend is that you start with…"

How to Overcome the Top Ten Objections in Sports Ticket Sales

Like all sales, when selling any kind of ticket or subscription events, you have the advantage because 90% of the time you know what most of the objections are going to be. Rarely are you going to get something you can't prepare for in advance, and by using, adapting, and practicing the scripts in this section, you'll be prepared to easily handle and overcome many of the objections that may be frustrating you now.

As always, spend some time with these scripts, adapt them to your particular team or event, and then make a commitment to using them. Just like any pro athlete, the more you practice perfection, the better, more instinctual, and more confident you'll become. Oh, and the more you'll win as well!

Objection #1: "The team stinks"

"_____, every team goes through cycles, but you know as well as I do that any game and any season can take on a life of its own. With all the new talent we've got this year (talk about new stars, new coaches, new philosophies), we're really excited about how this season is going to go, and where this team is headed in the future.

And don't forget that at any time we could get a world-class player that could change everything. This is why it makes sense to get your seats now before any big moves are made – does that make sense?

I understand, but don't forget the other reason you get season tickets – it gives you a regular opportunity to spend quality time with those you love. Let's face it, nothing is more fun than taking the family or friends to a sporting event. It's the memories that are made during these events that live on long past the season. And it's what sports are really all about.

Do yourself, your friends and your family a favor and get these seats while they are available, and lock in the good times and good memories now. Believe me, you'll always be glad you did..."

Objection #2: "We had to lay off people/can't justify the expense."

"Well, first of all, I'm sorry to hear that. But I'll tell you something – I work with companies all the time that have scaled back, or laid people off, and they all realize the same thing – now, more than ever, it's important to keep your remaining employees and customers feeling appreciated, happy and motivated. I'm sure you'd agree with that, wouldn't you?

And one of the best ways to do that is by investing in your season ticket plan. I mean, let me ask you – you're still investing in your business to make sure you stay competitive, keep your existing customers and attract new business, right? Well, one of the ways other companies do that is by keeping some of the perks that are crucial to accomplishing all of that. And that's where these tickets come in.

You see _____, nobody wants to work for a company they think is going out of business. And customers always want to do business with companies they see as successful and prosperous. The best way for you to project that image is to invest a little bit of money to keep your season ticket package together. Believe me, the little bit of money you'll spend here will go a long way toward getting and keeping the business that you need now more than ever. Here's what I recommend we do..."

Objection #3: "I'd rather purchase game-by-game."

"I know just what you mean. The disadvantage with that, of course, is that you never know what seats you'll end up with, and you'll almost always pay more than what I can give you today. And I'm sure you've experienced the hassle of buying individual seats, haven't you?

By being a season ticket holder _____, you can avoid all that. In addition, I can offer you:

- List your current benefits of buying season tickets with you today -

Pretty impressive, isn't it? You know you're going to games this season, and wouldn't you be happier knowing that you can go to any game you want, when you want to? Then let's do this..."

Objection #4: "Not in the budget/can't afford it."

"I totally understand. Let me ask you quickly, if you *could* afford to buy the seats you wanted, would you go ahead and do that today?"

- If no, then you've got other objections you need to deal with -

- If yes -

"Great! Then let me work with you on some options that may fit what you can afford today. First of all, we've got all kinds of packages available, so let me ask you – what price range would you want to look into – you know, what you might be able to afford if you really wanted to swing it this season?"

- Or -

"We have a lot of options available because we know how tight things are. For example, you could put a deposit down now to secure these seats, and then come up with the balance toward the start of the season. Many people get their friends or family members to chip in and that way they all get to some games and enjoy the season even more. Is that an option for you, too?"

- Or -

"You know, before you say no to what's going to be an exciting season, let me tell you about some of the more affordable options we have in place..."

- Or -

"_____, I'm sure you know of other people who would love to own these seats with you, so let me do this. I'll go ahead and put some packages together for you so you at least know what's available. That way, if something comes up, you'll know exactly what you can get, fair enough?"

Objection #5: "Too many games in the season."

"And that's actually what most people like about this. They like being able to pick and choose the games they go to and then split the other tickets with family, friends and business associates. How many games in a season would you plan to go to?

Great, then you can share the cost of the other tickets with people you know and still get to the games you want. Let's do this..."

- Or -

"There are just (X amount) of home games this year, and most of my clients use their extra seats as gifts for birthdays, or to reward employees or help build relationships with good prospects or clients. Believe me, you'll always find a good use for games you can't or don't want to attend, and having season tickets allows you to do that. Now, let's talk about a package that would be right for you..."

Objection #6: "I already have season tickets elsewhere."

"Of course you do! Most of our fans also own tickets elsewhere because they know and appreciate the benefits of being a season ticket holder. Plus, they like being able to choose which games/ sports to see depending on their schedule.

Besides, you probably have friends or business associates who like all kinds of different sports, right? Well, owning these tickets gives you the flexibility of a lot of different options. Plus, there are only (X number) of home games – it works out to about two a month, so there's very little conflict between what you're doing now. Let's talk about a package that might be right for you..."

Objection #7: "I'm not a fan of (sport)."

"_____, you don't have to be a fan of (your sport) to enjoy the experience of going to these games. They're great! The whole experience of getting together with good friends or family, being in the stadium and being a part of the event is worth everything.

Have you been to a (your sport or team) game lately? Things are much more exciting now with the entertainment, special promotions, and kids really have a great time. And I'll bet that while you may not be a big fan right now, I'm sure you know plenty of people who are, right? Having these season tickets is a great way to make a lot of people happy.

And _____, you probably know of some clients or people who you'd like to do business with who do like (this sport/team), right? Well, again, investing in these tickets is just another great way for you to strengthen and build those relationships. Do you think it might help you there?

Tell you what. Let's look at some of the great packages we've got available and find one that would work well for you and everyone else in your life who would enjoy this..."

Objection #8: "It's too far to go/I live too far away."

"_____, so many of my season ticket holders tell me that they look forward to spending the entire day enjoying these games. Their families look forward to it all week, and even when they have to drive to the games, it's time they get to spend together.

Besides that, when you're entertaining a business associate or prospect, going to the games gives you time to get to know more about them and their needs – it's time your competition never gets with them!

By the way, how many of these games would you be interested in attending in a season? Well that's great, because I'm sure you know other people who have an interest in attending games as well. Sharing the price with them is a great way to ensure that you and your family get to the games you really want to see. Now we have many packages available - what kind of price range are you looking for?"

Objection #9: "I don't like your coach/player(s)/owner/area."

"_____, I know what you mean – it's hard to like everybody on a team or in a company or even in a family – and I'm sure you know what I mean! But as you also know, a team isn't about an individual, it's about what it can do together – and that includes you, the fan. _____, how much fun do you have at games? And how much time do you spend during the week reading about them, talking to your friends about them or watching them on TV?

You see, what you know is true is that you enjoy the sport. You enjoy the competition. You probably enjoy the whole experience of participating in the event, don't you? Well, players/coaches/owners will come and go, but what is constant is our love of the game. And that's why people buy and hold onto season tickets. Let's talk about some options that would work for you..."

Objection #10: "I just lost my job/don't know if I'll have one later on."

"_____, let me ask you, are you independently wealthy?

- If no -

Then I can guarantee you you'll have another job again. And how long have you been a fan of (your team or sport)? OK, then I can also guarantee you that you'll want to be at the games this (coming season, or spring, etc.). You see, things may be tough temporarily, but they always turn around. Right now we've got all kinds of options to help you lock in your season tickets now, get the best seats available, and ensure that you get to keep enjoying the sport you love.

Plus, you can always share the expense with other fans and friends. Now let's look at a few options that you may be able to work into your existing budget..."

Bonus Section #6	# How to Overcome the Top Ten Objections in Merchant Services/ Credit Card Processing

The bankcard industry is a highly competitive and, some would say, saturated industry. Each month, merchants receive hundreds of calls from would-be processing companies claiming to save them money on their monthly processing fees. The problem, of course, is that each time you drop your rate, you drop your profit margin, and if you're selling on rates alone, then you always stand the chance of someone calling right behind you and dropping their rates as well.

The answer in today's market is to offer more than just rates, and that, of course, is to offer a business some true added value. There are many new products available to help merchants grow and improve their businesses. Your competitive advantage is in engaging the merchant and showing them how you, and you alone, have the solutions for their problems. As always, it's about creating a relationship and building trust.

The rebuttals below are geared toward allowing you to deal with the reflex responses you get when calling merchants. They are structured to help you get your foot in the door – in other words, they are written to help you engage with the merchant and to get to that first stage: Having them trust you enough to send you their statements so you can go to work to build value in your products and services.

Have these rebuttals next to the phone when making cold calls, and be sure to adjust them to fit your products, personality and market you are calling into.

Objection #1 "I have a contract"

"That's exactly why I'm calling. You see most people we work with have a contract as well. But the bottom line is that we offer our clients so much more value than they are used to getting, as well as save them as much as 20 – 30%, that you're going to want to look at what we can do for you, too. Quick question: How much are you currently processing now per month?"

- If they don't want to say -

"No problem, let me ask you this then, on average, how much are you paying now for your total processing fees?"

- Cancellation fee objection -

"Of course you do, and our rates can be so much lower that you can often recoup that fee in less than three months – and the savings after that are all profit for you. Does that make sense?"

- Or -

"We've developed a program that rebates back to you up to $295.00 to be applied to your cancellation fee. So why don't we take the first step and see how much value we can add to your business, as well as how much we can save you. Does that make sense?"

Objection #2 "I process with my bank"

"That's great! We work with your bank as well. The only difference is, we save you money on the front end. Let me ask you – if I could show you how to save as much as 20%-30% per month in fees, not change your banking relationship, and give you technology and value that will actually add to your business, is that something you'd at least be interested in learning more about?"

- Or -

"What most people don't understand is that your bank doesn't do the processing, just the collecting – so they're not concerned with saving you money and they're certainly not that good at adding value to your business – that's my job. Let me ask you this – if I could save you up to 50% in fees each month on your processing volume while adding some real value to your business - and still have your bank do the collecting - would you be interested in learning more about it?"

Objection #3 "I'm not interested"

"I didn't expect you to be. I'm sure you get a ton of these kinds of calls, and I'm sure you're sick of hearing how everybody can save you money, right? Well _____, this isn't one of those calls and I'll tell you why: While I can probably save you money as well, what's important is how I can add real value to your business, and give you tools and technology that will actually help it run better.

What I'd suggest for you is to learn what I can do for you, and, yes, even learn about how we can also save you money each month, and then you'll be in a better position to decide if it's worth it to make a change. Does that make sense to you?"

- Or -

"I wouldn't be either until I knew I could save more money each month and get some real value out of making that change. Let me ask you a quick question: Would you at least be open to a review of how I can add value to your business and give you a free, layer by layer comparison to see how much more money you could put in your pocket each month by putting us to work for you?"

Objection #4 "I'm happy with my current processor"

"Great, what makes you so happy with them?"

- If they love the rates -

"That's great and let me ask you this – how much happier would you be if we could save you as much as 20-30% on your monthly fees?"

- Or -

"If you like your service now, then you'll love the added value and technology that comes with our service. In fact, when you hear about what we can do to help your business grow, you'll be happy you took a moment to listen. Let me ask you a quick question about your business…"

Objection #5 "Tell me your rate."

"You know _____, whenever someone says that to me, it tells me they don't fully understand how processing works. Most merchants tell their customers they're paying one rate, but that can be misleading...

In fact, did you know that when you're paying only one rate, your processor will charge you a higher rate or a cushion to ensure costs for all cards are covered?

_____, Visa and MasterCard have different rates for each transaction type and when I see your statements, you may be surprised by how much you're paying, and by how much we can save you! But that's just the start, because there's so much more value you should be getting from your processing company.

Let's do this. I'll ask you just a couple of quick questions about what you do and then I'll let you know how I might be able to help you – fair enough?"

Objection #6 "I'm fine where I am"

"I'm sure you are, and you probably felt that way before you changed to your current processor - and most people I speak with are. But there have been some big changes in the bankcard industry, and there are many technology changes and value-added options that many clients are missing out on.

Let me ask you this: If I could find a way to bring some real value to your business and even save you some money, wouldn't it at least be in your best interest to learn more about it?

Let's do this – I'll ask you just a couple of quick questions about how you do business and if I find that I can help you, I'll give you some ideas. If not, then I'll tell you you've got a good deal now. Is that fair enough?

Objection #7 "Send me information, and I will compare it to my current statement"

"I would be happy to do that, and I'll even go further and do the work for you. Tell you what - I want you to be able to compare apples to apples, and I want you to know exactly what you'll save by going with our program. Moreover, it's important for you to know about the current value-added features you could be using to make more money in your business.

Here's what you should do: Go ahead and fax me over your last two months' statements and I'll give you a direct comparison of what you're paying and what you're getting in return for that. If, after I see it, I find that you're already getting a better deal, I'll tell you. And if we can save you money and give you some benefits that will help you even more, I'll tell you that as well. Either way, you'll win. Does that sound fair?"

Objection #8 "I don't have time to look at my statement"

"No problem - let me do that for you. I can prepare an accurate analysis of your current processor with an apples to apples look at the current fees and, more importantly, the current benefits available to you, and then present it back to you. We can meet for a few minutes by phone or I can even send it back via e-mail or fax.

Believe me _____, the small amount of time invested to review your current fees and features in comparison with what I may be able to offer you could mean a lot to your business. If you have a pen handy, I'll be glad to give you my fax number..."

Objection #9 "We process through an association program"

"That's great, in fact I work with a lot of companies that are in association programs and the reason they're interested in our program is they are often over paying because the association's one rate applies to all members.

Did you know that since Visa and MasterCard have different rates based on industry type and how cards are processed, one-rate programs can sometimes end up costing you more in processing fees?

You see, these are just some of the things you need to know about in order to do what's best for your company. Here's what I recommend – go ahead and send me two months' worth of statements and I'll do a direct comparison across all categories – including some of the rebates and features that are now available to you. When I'm done I'll let you know if we can help you. Do you have a pen handy?"

Objection #10 "We already pay below 1%"

"_____, I find that a lot of the time, my merchants look at one rate, but it turns out that only a small portion of their business is being processed at that rate. A lot of it is processed at a higher rate of three or even four percent!

Tell you what I'll do: I'll be happy to go over your statement and tell you for sure what you're paying. If you're getting a good deal, then

I'll tell you. If I can save you money each month, I'll tell you that, too.

More importantly, there are many new features that we offer companies that can save them a lot more than just money – and you need to know about them. I'll take the time to give you an up-to-date analysis on what you're paying and what's available to you. After you see it in writing, you can make a decision as to what's best for your business. Is that fair?"

Acknowledgements

Someone asked me how long it took to write this book of phone scripts, and my initial answer was two years. But when I gave it more thought, I realized it has taken over 20 years! It was during these 20 years that I first learned to use scripts to begin with, learned to trust them and stick to them, learned to adapt them and adjust them to the various products and prospects I've worked with during my career.

Over the years I've been influenced by countless sales managers, sales trainers, sales reps and motivational speakers, and all of them have influenced the writing of this book. I'd like to take a moment now to acknowledge a few of them, but please note that the following is in no way an exhaustive list of the time, effort and patience that has been extended to me during my career of selling over the phone.

To start with, I want to acknowledge the enormous amount of work that has been done on this manuscript by my publisher and friend, Jeb Blount, and his team at Sales Gravy Press. Jeb, I know how much work, how many hours, and how much of yourself you have put into this book. I deeply appreciate you and your belief in my work, and I am continually grateful for all the time and effort you put into my projects through Salesgravy.com. Thank you for everything you do!

Next I would like to thank my brother, Peter Brooks (my first sales manager) for teaching how to use scripts to truly listen to what my prospects were trying to tell me. This has been an invaluable skill that I try to teach to others.

I'd also like to acknowledge the first two big influences on my selling styles and career: The first is Mr. Fantastic himself, Stan Billue. Stan, your cassette series was the best training tool I had for many years, and in it I learned the value of following a proven system. Next I'd like to thank the first motivational speaker I ever heard – Bob Mowad of the Edge Learning Institute. Bob's material was instrumental in helping me transform myself from the inside out, and I owe a giant part of my overall success to this day to the training and teaching he delivered to me all those years ago.

I also want to thank Jennie Romer for her intensive editing job late in the process. Thank you for being there for me when I needed you and for doing such an excellent job as always!

Next, I'd like to acknowledge some of my clients for taking the time to read the early manuscript and for your excellent comments and support. In particular, I'd like to thank Kevin Gaither, Shon Messer, and Jim Facente.

In addition, I'd like to thank Judy Slack at Tom Hopkins International for working so hard to get this to Tom, and to Jeannette Dolis at Brian Tracy's office for getting this to Brian. I appreciate your help and your belief in my work.

Finally, I'd like to thank all the sales reps over the years with whom I've worked. It's your persistence, hard work, and willingness to make just one more call that has motivated me to write and publish this book of scripts. I've enjoyed working with you all, and I look forward to meeting and helping thousands of more sales reps become Top 20% producers.

About Mike Brooks, Mr. Inside Sales

Mr. Inside Sales (aka Mike Brooks), has been called upon by companies and individuals alike to move their sales out of the 80% and into the Top 20%. He has over 25 years of inside sales closing experience. Once a bottom 80% producer, Mike learned and perfected the skills of Top 20% producers and became the number one sales rep out of five Southern California branch offices.

Author of the international weekly Ezine, "Inside Sales Secrets of the Top 20%," and author of the best selling book, *Real Secrets of the Top 20%*, Mike's proven techniques, strategies and skills are used successfully by companies in industries such as securities sales, high-tech sales, pharmaceuticals, equipment leasing, and other business-to-business applications.

Mike combines proven, current tactics and skills with personal experience to provide a motivational and practical presentation.

For more information on having Mike present a customized training program to your company, call:

1-818-999-0869 or visit www.MrInsideSales.com

CPSIA information can be obtained at www.ICGtesting.com
Printed in the USA
LVOW11s2253140716

496351LV00001B/54/P